The *Back-to-Front* Boy

The *Back-to-Front* Boy

A true story of adopting a boy
with attachment disorder

Rebecca Wright

Covenanters

Published by
Covenanters Press

the joint imprint of
Zeticula
57 St Vincent Crescent
Glasgow
G3 8NQ
and
Scottish Christian Press
21 Young Street
Edinburgh
EH2 4HU

http://www.covenanters.co.uk
admin@covenanters.co.uk

Illustrations © Katherine Wake 2004
Cover design by Heather Macpherson

ISBN 1 905022 09 3 Paperback
ISBN 1 905022 10 7 Hardback

Foreword
Caroline Archer

This short book by Rebecca Wright provides a warm and very realistic picture of the ups and downs of adoptive family life. It is clear that the author (and her husband) have never lost their sense of humour – without that all three lives may have turned out quite differently.

The past decade has brought powerful ammunition from the neurobiological sciences to support what I, at Adoption UK and as an independent Parent Mentor, have believed for much longer: that the developmental consequences of very early maltreatment can be pervasive, affecting a child's functioning not just in social relationships but also in the physical, emotional, intellectual and spiritual dimensions of their lives. Sadly, difficulties in each of these areas tend to be approached from different directions, as we hear in Sam's story, with the 'big picture' tending to go unrecognised. However, without a developmental understanding of the effects of poor attachment experiences and early traumatic events in young children's lives it is not possible to understand 'why they are like they are and why they do what they do'. We then have our hands tied when it comes to meeting their needs in the most effective and appropriate ways.

A myth appears to pervade our collective social conscience that pre-school children who are placed for adoption will soon settle down and be able to benefit from the enhanced opportunities they are offered in their new homes and communities. Increasingly, over time, I have seen that this expectation is not only unrealistic but unfair to the child and his committed parents – who often end up having to use vital energy 'fighting the system' on his behalf; vital energy that could better be channelled into supporting him.

In this story, which manages to remain heart-warming and hopeful despite the obvious and continuing struggles, there are so many clues that let us know that Sam's neurological development did not go well, leaving him with some degree of neurobiological disorganisation. Without knowing Sam's very early history I can only guess at what interruptions to his attachment and developmental pathways took place; that they did take place I have no doubt. For this story bears out what I have learned from my own experiences of adoptive parenting and from supporting adoptive and foster families, that 'children who hurt' frequently continue to struggle at many levels within even the most caring and creative substitute families. Time and love helps but does not heal all the wounds; some mountains remain unassailed!

Theraplay, in the United States, and the Developmental Reparenting strategies developed through Adoption UK and made accessible to families through Family Futures and Holding Families Together, offer us greater hope for the future. Taking a developmentally informed approach to reparenting traumatised children, parents, with the right information and support, can move 'bigger mountains' with and for their child. Now the onus is on placing agencies to take up the challenge and begin to make more sophisticated assessments of the child's global needs prior to placement. An integrated multi-disciplinary post adoption support system must also be established across the UK so that every adoptive family has access to the information and help they need to make them positive agents for change in their children's lives from 'Day 1'. Only in that way can future 'Sam families' channel their raw commitment and energies into enabling their children to reach their optimal potential *with* the support of child care, education, psychological and health services, rather than in spite of it!

I congratulate Rebecca on her openness, candour and humour. Without her, and her husband's, patent good sense, endurance and capacity to go on taking up the challenge, Sam wouldn't be where he is today. Well done Sam for hanging in there and doing so well. Keep up the good work and thank you all for daring to share your lives with us!

Caroline Archer
September 2004

Chapter 1

The door was opened by a breathless, small, attractive blonde boy with piercing blue eyes, the rosiest cheeks you ever did see and a big wide smile. He didn't stop long enough to hear our names, or even why we were there, because he dashed off again as if on an urgent mission. "So you've met 'im then?" foster mum enquired with a raucous laugh as she led us into the big square family kitchen, just in time to see Sam scrambling down from the kitchen work top with a cold roast potato left over from Sunday lunch. "'E's a little divil!" she exclaimed in exasperation. "The number of times 'e's been told to leave them cold roasties alone," she said shaking her head in disbelief at her lack of success in controlling him.

"Doin' a brew mother?" enquired a large teenage boy with a lumberjack shirt and socks with massive holes in each toe. "He's messin' wi' t' video again mother," he informed us as he sloped back into the lounge giving us a cursory nod as he went.

"Dave!" she shouted at the top of her voice, "Can you watch him please while I make a brew for Rebecca and John? That video has only just come back from the menders," she told us in a conspiratorial whisper. "I've told 'em at Social Services that they'll have to pay for the next repair because there's no way we can afford this! You've only got to take your eyes off 'im for a minute and 'e's into something else. I tell you, I've been fostering now for six years and I ain't ever had one like this before and that's the truth," she said in real earnest. "I've only had 'im these six months and 'e's making me ill," she huffed and puffed as she made the tea, "Mind, I've 'ad Jackie for the last two weeks like, and that's been a big help," she continued as she tipped some biscuits onto a plate. "I've to 'ide these from 'im or he'd 'av 'em all," she declared with glee as if she'd finally managed to pull a fast one and defeat him in the biscuit wars.

"Who's Jackie?" I ventured, as she carried the tea tray through to the sitting room which contained the rest of the family.

"Oh, she's the Family Aid, that Social Services sent me when I told 'em that he was getting me down like," she informed me in her West Country accent.

As we entered the small but cosy sitting room the television dominated the room and despite the brilliant sunshine the curtains were drawn.

"'Ow do." The three big bulky men on the settee nodded to us as we sat down balancing our cups of strong tea on our knees, their eyes immediately drawn back to the shooting, fighting and galloping on offer on the enormous screen in the corner.

"My lads love their Sunday westerns, they're like their dad," foster mum commented with pride as she fondly looked across at the three men, all of the same build, all with massive holes in their socks and wiggling their toes in contentment as they settled down to enjoy their favourite time of the week, prospective adopters or not!

A little ginger and white bear came hurtling through the air at such a speed that I didn't see it until it was too late and the strong hot tea had begun to soak into my skirt.

"That's 'im showing off," commented foster mum with exasperation. "You're not takin' enough notice of 'im like, and that's 'is way of telling you 'e's 'ere! 'Ere, what's 'e been doin' behind that fish tank?" she asked in panic as foster dad jumped up quickly to protect his beloved fish.

"Little devil's only gone and emptied half a tub of

'Guppie' in t' water!" Dave declared in disgust, as a flash of blonde dashed past out of the door and up the stairs.

"'E's as 'igh as a kite," Julie offered by way of explanation as we sat looking bemused at the unfolding spectacle. "'E's 'ad a lot of people looking at 'im over the past few weeks and although we've told 'im they're our friends, 'e's not stupid like," she declared with insight, "'E knows why they're 'ere." At three and a half Sam had just been freed for adoption, which was why we were there, the idea being to go and watch him interact within a normal family with the possibility of us taking him on as prospective adopters.

His constant hypervigilance and hyperactivity were apparently symptomatic of his lack of security, uncertainty and understanding about what was happening. Sam had been taken away from his birth parent as a baby and was now on his second set of foster parents, the first being considered too inexperienced, having 'cut their teeth' on Sam and in doing so failing to pick up on a language delay. Consequently he had been moved on to Julie and Dave, in the hope that more experienced foster parents might accelerate his progress. It was daunting to say the least to realise that even an experienced foster mum was finding him hard work. It was noticeable that all the time she was discreetly trying to fill us in on confidential past history, Sam kept tabs on us by tearing back into the sitting room to check that we were still there, before racing off again to play with foster brothers upstairs who represented security and familiarity. At one point during the afternoon I was aware of a small blue eye watching me very closely through the crack in the sitting room door, but as soon as he knew I had seen him, he darted away to avoid any chance of interaction.

Interaction between us wasn't long in coming,

however, when we went to sit down in the kitchen for tea. As is traditional in some west country households, the trifle is eaten before the sandwiches. I found myself next to Sam, and it wasn't long before he was depositing all the fruit cocktail from his trifle onto my plate! This wasn't an easy task as his spoon was in one hand and the small ginger bear was grasped tightly in the other.

Ginger bear had been given to Sam by his birth mother on the last occasion that she had seen him, and although he came in for a lot of biting, thumping, kicking and throwing, the bear was always by Sam's side at bedtime and never far away during the day. I couldn't help but notice that Sam's first meal with us consisted of only one half-eaten sandwich; the rest was pure sugar in the form of biscuits, buns and half-eaten slices of cake.

Determined that we should share a book together before we went home, Sam and I sat at the kitchen table after the tea things had been cleared away."What 'dat?" were Sam's first words to me as I produced a *Thomas the Tank Engine* 'Lift the Flap' book from a paper bag.

"Oh, 'e don't like books," said foster mum. "Only thing 'e likes to do with 'em is throw 'em!"

Keeping a tight grip on the cardboard book, I showed Sam how to lift the flap once we had read the sentence on the page. Within minutes, reading the book had turned into a battle, with Sam trying to lift the flap before we had read the sentence. Neither was he bothered about the order in which he read it and seemed determined to start from the back and work his way forwards. After establishing that we were going to read it properly and in the right order, in frustration and sensing a moment of weakness, he seized the opportunity to grab the book and hurl it across the room.

"There you are, I told 'e he don't like books!" said foster mum, trying to keep the "I told you so" out of her voice.

It was at this point that we decided that a walk outside might be a good idea. This gave Sam the opportunity to sit on the bottom of the stairs and wiggle his feet at me saying, "Beck do it." Once his shoes were tied and his wax jacket admired and fastened up we set off. The west country village was small but picturesque and once we had enjoyed a game of catch around the war memorial we began to feel we were doing quite well. We had decided to walk to the bridge and float twigs and leaves on the stream when we were forced to squeeze into the edge of the lane to allow an enormous tractor to pass by. As the huge wheels rolled past covered in mud, I couldn't help but look at Sam to gauge his reaction, was he frightened by its size or fascinated? He was neither, I watched as he raised his hand in a friendly wave at the driver, quickly followed by a thumbs up sign. Foster mum laughed at my surprise to see a little three year old on such friendly terms with a tractor driver.

"Dave knows most of the drivers in the village and Sam thinks he does too," she said by means of explanation, but what this didn't explain was why he did it to nearly every passing vehicle, be it a tractor or not! Most drivers responded to him with a smile and often a thumbs up back, as the sight of a friendly little blonde three year old was endearing. Safety was definitely something we were going to have to think about in the future, I thought to myself as we continued on our walk.

We noticed that a lot of the cottages were thatched and that on the top of some of them the thatcher had left his trade-mark, a little bird made of straw.

"Look," I said to Sam as I pointed skywards, "Look at that little bird." I wasn't ready for the response I got.

"Bang! Bang!" he shouted at the top of his voice accompanied by the action of firing a shotgun. I was shocked by this seemingly brutal response.

"Come on Sam," interjected Julie, " Let's go and see the moo cows." I realised later that this was her way of trying to distract Sam from the sticky subject of guns, which were kept safely and securely padlocked in a cupboard in the kitchen. They were used for shooting crows and pigeons from farmers' fields and although Dave had a licence and all was above board and legal, they seemed to provide an endless source of fascination for Sam, who, at a later date, had grabbed John by the hand, led him to the particular cupboard in question and said, "Look, bang bangs!"

After a short trek across the road and up a lane we all ended up staring at an empty field. The cows were missing!

"That's funny," said Julie, "It isn't time for milking yet, I wonder where they are?"

"All dead!" explained Sam, "Gone!" His brutal explanation of the disappearance of the cows made me wonder if he associated the sudden disappearance of all things with death. I couldn't help but wonder, rightly or wrongly, if he thought that this was the explanation for the disappearance of his birth mother.

We decided to end the outing on a more positive note by suggesting a trip to the village sweet shop. Sam was down the lane like greased lightning as he and the sweet shop lady were well acquainted. Julie was determined that he should spend his own money and that one thing was enough. Sam chose a lollipop and a bar of chocolate.

"No, Sam, I said one thing," said foster mum firmly, clearly determined to show that she stood no messing about. After a mega tantrum and the chocolate bar being forced out of Sam's hand and put back on a low shelf Sam appeared to be distracted by having to hand over the money for the lollipop himself. It was while foster mum was having a friendly word with the shopkeeper that I noticed Sam's hand sneak out and help himself to the mangled chocolate bar he had been forced to return! Clearly there was a lot of work ahead, if we decided to proceed with the placement.

Chapter 2

We looked at the list again and sighed.

"There certainly appear more *cons* than *pros*," said John as we both analysed the things for and against taking on board a hyperactive three and a half year old.

"*Cons*," read out John with resignation, " Language delay, learning delay, hyperactivity, lack of boundaries, doesn't understand the word 'NO'!"

"*Pros*," I interjected quickly, Sam's cheeky face and blue mischievous eyes dancing in front of me for a split second, "Friendly, affectionate, attractive, fun?" I suggested hopefully.

Sam's language and learning delay had been explained by lack of attachment in his early years to an adult; emotional trauma and lack of consistent boundaries. These problems would, we were assured, be helped by a consistent and secure home life.

"All he needs is a mum and dad," we had been told by his Social Worker.

"What really bothers me," mused John, "is our ability to keep him safe. He's going to take so much watching. He's going to need six Norland Nannies all to himself, working on a strict rota system day and night!" he said sarcastically. "And, as we can't even afford one, we are going to be absolutely exhausted all the time. It's goodbye to life as we know it," he added gloomily.

The telephone rang shrilly. Distractedly I picked it up.

"Beck come. You come, see me!" it was Sam. We took a deep breath and started to plan our second visit.

As we walked up the path, the bright wintry sunshine shone down on us, almost as if in encouragement. We began to feel quietly optimistic about our planned afternoon at the seaside as we made our way up the path in between the plastic wheelbarrows and toy cars. Before we even had time to knock, the door was swung open by Sam. "You comed!" he said triumphantly and then ran off down the hall at full pelt.

"He's been so excited all morning," said Julie. "I could hardly get him to eat his dinner, didn't even eat all his roasties!" she added with a laugh as she struggled to get him into his blue wax jacket.

"Want Beck do it!" Sam interjected suddenly. I was shocked by the apparent attachment that he already seemed to be making with us. I was beginning to feel that I was losing control as I contemplated the possible scenario of him wanting us, but us not wanting him. His extreme vulnerability suddenly hit me, and I fought back the tears as we retraced our steps back down the garden path. As soon as he saw the bright red Honda he wanted to sit on John's knee and pretend to drive. John indulged him for a few minutes until Sam's attention was distracted by the switches on the dashboard. "What dat for?" was his constant question, the windscreen wipers being a particular source of amusement. After switching them on and off at least ten times John firmly removed his hands.

"More screen-winds!" Sam shouted in dismay as John started the car and put on the playgroup songtime tape.

Foster mum had warned us about the difficult job of keeping his seatbelt on in the car and had treated us to numerous horror stories of only being able to take him out in twos, one driving while the other rode shotgun in the back. Our solution to this problem had been to distract him with story tapes and songs that he might know from playgroup. At first, on hearing the happy jaunty music, Sam sat still, alert, listening. "Where dat from?" he asked having studied John and myself carefully to make sure that we weren't the perpetrators.

"It's nice music," volunteered John, " Come on let's join in!" he said with gusto, but Sam was having none of it.

"Where dat from?" he asked again twisting himself around trying to find the source of the noise.

"It's from the tape recorder at the front of the car Sam," I explained, sensing his confusion.

"Look," said John tapping it to prove a point.

Sam was relentless in pursuing an explanation which satisfied him.

"Where dat lady?" he kept asking as he swivelled either side in his car seat to try to spot her.

"It's the speakers in the back of the car, he thinks there's a lady in the back singing!" I suddenly realised.

"Look, Sam, it's the speakers," I said as I leant forwards tapping them loudly to help him to understand.

"No, want see lady singing," he insisted obviously getting quite agitated, so we pulled over and stopped. I unclipped his seat belt and immediately Sam proceeded to do a scrupulous inspection of the car, which the local drugs squad would have been proud of. "In boot!" he commanded John as he led me from the back seat and round to the back of the car. John dutifully released the boot, knowing when he was beaten, and Sam proceeded to climb over the tailgate and into the boot to continue his relentless search for the lady. Realising that there was no way we were going to get to the seaside at this rate, John had the foresight to turn the tape off.

"Lady gone now!" Sam exclaimed with satisfaction, rubbing his hands together like an old man. "All gone now. Dead!" Oh no, not that old chestnut again! My emotions plummeted and I felt my earlier optimism begin to disappear.

It was a relief to get to the sea as I had become tired of the game Sam had concocted of seatbelts on, seatbelts off.

"Everybody out!" ordered John with a voice full of optimism in order to introduce a more positive note to the afternoon. "Let's have a game of chase!" he shouted picking up a piece of seaweed and holding it behind him like a tail. "Bet you can't get my tail, Sam," he challenged, trying to run off some of the petulance that had built up by the end of the journey. Sam didn't need asking twice. He was off, running this way and that, laughing and loving every minute of the fun. John was deliberately teasing him by letting him get as close as possible and then running away. Sam's obvious enjoyment was catching and soon I became aware of a small group of old age pensioners smiling indulgently at the little boy. Sam's cheeks were positively glowing and his eyes were sparkling. I began to relax, all worries about him coping away from foster mum for the first time vanishing.

After the game, Sam decided to do a bit of digging, not with the buckets and spades we had carefully packed for him but with his hands together, like a big scoop throwing the sand behind him and through his legs like an excited dog retrieving a bone. Sand was flying everywhere and the activity became frantic and out of control. Other parents were looking in disgust now at the naughty three year old.

"Stop it, Sam!" I commanded. "It's going in people's eyes!" Too late, I got a mouthful of sand and I began to feel furious at being ignored by him and embarrassed at being judged as an ineffective parent by the pensioners sitting on the bench. John had thought more quickly than I and was approaching him from the front. He grabbed him around the waist, turned him upside down and turned what could have been a confrontation into a new game of swinging him round holding his knees, Sam's arms outstretched as if in freefall.

"More, more!" he demanded as John tried to regain his balance after giving him about ten twirls.

"Come on, let's skim some stones," I suggested, trying to distract him, running down the pebbly beach in the hope that he would follow.

"No, Sam, skim like this, don't throw," I tried to show him the difference but it was no good.

"Throw them into the sea!" I commanded when the stones started to fly behind, to the side, above, anywhere but in front of us. Sam was having a lovely time and there was no way he was going to let anyone stop him. John came to the rescue with his seaweed tail.

"Can't get me!" he teased wiggling it like mad and ran off up the beach closely followed by Sam.

It was at this point that one of the pensioners sitting on the bench decided to interject.

"Eeh lad," he volunteered in a thick Barnsley accent, "If I were thee, I'd tie 'im to that post and gerr 'off t'pub for a pint. It meks mi tired just watching thee!" It was at this point we realised that we had been providing entertainment for two benches of Yorkshire pensioners who were at great pains to point out how much easier it had been to be a parent in their day when you could

"Give 'em a good belt and 'av done wi' it!"

We took their advice about the refreshments but not the punishment, and retired to a pretty little tea shop. This was 'done out' with lace at the windows, high backed church pews for seats and, running across the tops of the pews, brass poles with silly bits of lace attached to the underside in an attempt to make each customer's table private. Once our order had been taken it was good to be out of the wind and the sun and take in our surroundings. Sam had other ideas. The sugar bowl became a source of fascination as he began to dig into it with the sugar spoon as if looking for buried treasure. The sugar tongs were intriguing and Sam picked up the brown sugar cubes and methodically placed them in the loose white sugar bowl so by the time the waitress brought the tea, the table looked like an explosion on a building site. She tutted as she attempted to wipe away our mess and place the tea things on the table.

Sam's chocolate milkshake came complete with long handled spoon and so, after his thirst had been quenched he proceeded to ladle the remaining sticky brown liquid from his tall glass into the empty milk jug, pouring the then chocolatey milk into our empty tea cups and back again. By the time the waitress had brought the cake it looked as though the Aswan Dam had burst its banks.

Again she showed her annoyance by commenting that she would have to go and get another cloth. As soon as the table had been cleaned and order restored, Sam began to get restless and decided that he could have a really interesting game of hide-and-seek with the two old ladies having afternoon tea in the pew behind us. He proceeded to stand on the seat and pull the lace curtain backwards and forwards, grinning at them, and then hiding before he thought they could see him. He was thoroughly absorbed in this game and was getting over-excited by it, basking in the success of having invented it himself, when one old lady was heard commenting to the other,

"Thoroughly spoilt, I've been watching him, no discipline at all! He'll be their one and only!"

It was obvious that the misconceptions, misunderstandings and judgements by others had begun.

Chapter 3

"And I am 95% certain that this hyperactivity is not organic," the child psychiatrist stated very firmly as we both leant forwards to take in his every word. I began to wish that I'd brought my tape recorder so that I could play it back to myself on bad days!

"What do you mean by organic?" I asked the balding doctor; I couldn't for the life of me get this image of organic eggs with lions stamped on them out of my head.

"Not inbuilt, not part of him," he explained patiently and quietly as if my own mental state was questionable and I had to be treated very carefully.

"So you mean we're not looking at Attention Deficit Hyperactivity Disorder then?" I asked carefully. We were already beginning to get used to all the jargon associated with children with Special Needs.

"As I said before, I think that is extremely unlikely. I think that we are looking at Attachment Disorder which mirrors ADHD in its symptoms, which are, in Sam's case, hyperactivity, impulsiveness, difficulty accepting boundaries and authority." He stopped there, watching our faces change as the list went on. "You have to realise that you are taking on a difficult child here. Your life for the next eighteen months or two years is going to be completely taken over by Sam."

He paused to give us time to assimilate the enormity of what he had just said, then he added most sincerely, "I have two birth children, one two and one six months and they have completely taken over our lives. Sam is going to be much more demanding even though there is only one of him," he paused, then said, "I'm not sure I could do it."

I was so grateful for his honesty in making us realise the enormity of what were about to take on and in admitting that, despite his obvious professional skills, even he would find the task daunting.

"Thank you for being so honest," I whispered as we made our way out of the room, my heart had pitched at his last comment and I was beginning to feel unsure that we were doing the right thing in proceeding with the placement of Sam with us.

Julie's struggle in managing Sam's behaviour had resulted in Social Services providing two additional means of support, one in the home in the form of Jackie, the Family Aid and the other in the form of Child Guidance. We were particularly anxious to seek the professional opinion of the child psychiatrist before we decided to proceed any further. Our Social Worker, an exceptionally sympathetic lady who was married to a vicar, had been listening in at the interview. I mused on how little times had changed in some ways as vicars' wives have traditionally gone around the parish doing good. This was obviously still happening today, the only difference being that she was now getting paid for it, so I decided to take her up on her offer of buying the coffees while we dissected in more detail what the psychiatrist had said.

"It's going to be tough for the first couple of years," said John, sounding much more positive than I felt, " But what really makes me optimistic is the fact he thinks his behaviour will improve even though it will be hard on us at first." This was the beginning of a pattern that was to establish itself over the next few years which actually helped to get us through. When one of us was down, the other was always up. It was like climbing a steep mountain, taking it in turns to haul each other up until we reached the top, except that when we got there we realised that there was always another summit to climb, but maybe that was just part of being a parent, birth parent or otherwise?

Once we had made the decision to proceed with 'the placement,' an official term used when a child is placed within a family with a view to adoption, we felt it important to get the neighbours on our side. Like many people nowadays, we lived on a new estate where the houses were built close together and where the roads were narrow to discourage people using them as 'rat runs.' People could quite clearly see into each other's gardens, many of which were open plan at the front having wide tarmac drives to allow for the parking of two cars.

The neighbours on either side and across the road were invited round and treated to a slideshow of Sam on the swings, Sam on the slide, Sam with his wheelbarrow, in order to explain the sudden appearance of this hyperactive three year old in a week's time. It was one of the best ideas we ever had. Volunteers to babysit flooded in from the couple with the immaculate bungalow across the road. They had three grand children, of whom they never saw enough because they lived so far away. The part-time teacher from next door, who had two boys herself, thought Sam looked wonderful and said that he could go round to play anytime. She also promised that she would get her boys to go through their cupboards and route out all their old toys for him. The enthusiasm was almost tangible and for that we were so grateful, as we had no immediate family in the West Country and help was going to be essential.

It appeared that at last, we were now going to become a family. After years of disappointment trying for a family of our own, followed by unsuccessful fertility treatment, our despair over an unfulfilled future had changed, and it seemed that our dream was about to come true.

Sam was unsure about wanting to come with us on the day we finally collected him for good. We were to become his fourth set of parents in three and a half years, just when he had finally begun to feel settled with Julie and her two boys. He openly called her "mummy" and there were tears all round as she tried to encourage him to get into the car. He had been on short visits before we had made the decision to proceed and Julie had explained this by telling him that he was going on his holidays, but this time he knew it was for real. He clung to her and I felt desperately inadequate as I tried to excite him with tales of chocolate cakes that had been baked for a special tea and how the boys next door were looking forward to meeting him and playing with him. I envied the effortless "motherliness" of Julie and began to feel inferior in my mothering skills. She always knew what to say, when to react and when to ignore certain behaviours and I knew that Sam was going to miss her maturity and reassurance. So was I! All was silent in the car until Sam cut across the silence by asking,

"Why did mummy give me away?"

I was shocked by the brutal way in which he seemed to judge relationships and spent the rest of the journey trying to reassure him that Julie would be coming to see us soon to check that he was all right and that he was getting "plenty of cups of tea"- Julie's own words - as she loved endless supplies of tea. I kept re-iterating that Julie wasn't 'a keeping mummy,' a term Social Services had told us to use when trying to explain the transfer from Foster Carer to Prospective Adopters. By the time we got home we were all emotionally exhausted.

My neighbour was true to her word and came round

with her two boys to welcome Sam. They had a special "Welcome Present" for him wrapped up in shiny paper. It was a soft friendly looking little hedgehog which Sam hugged with over-the-top affection. He promptly placed it next to his ginger bear, which was never far from his side, and then proceeded to be distracted by the toys that the boys had rooted out of their toy box as promised. Storing these toys was going to be a challenge; the house had very little space, so we had bought a large pink blanket box which co-ordinated nicely with my lounge. At the time, in my pre-Sam days, this seemed really important!

Sam however had other uses for the toy box and on one very wet Sunday very shortly after he had come to stay, he decided that it would be much more fun to use it as a hiding place. All the toys were emptied out of the box and spread around the lounge floor, while Sam jumped inside and banged the lid shut. At first we played along with him but after ten minutes we had truly had enough of the constant thumping and crashing of the lid. Despite numerous efforts to distract him - he wasn't going to let a pair of boring adults spoil his new game - Sam took no notice. Removal to his bedroom usually resulted in a tantrum with walls being kicked, books being thrown and Sam completely losing control. We wanted to avoid this at all costs, so John decided to distract him by taking him out in the rain. Boots were pulled on, wax jackets were fastened, golf umbrellas found and then they were both ready. Up and down the street they ran, hopped, jumped with feet together, skipped, anything to tire out a hyperactive three year old. The rain still poured, curtains twitched as neighbours watched the spectacle with indulgence and a wry smile, but no-one volunteered to come and help out! Suddenly Sam lost interest - he had seen a brave old lady tottering down the street bent against the wind and rain. He was off running towards her as if he knew her. What on earth was he going to do? I thought to myself.

"Sam, come back!" John was shouting, worried that he might suddenly run into the road. I knew him well enough to know that he wouldn't listen. If Sam wanted to do something, there was nothing anyone could do to stop him. As soon as he got close enough he launched himself on the old lady and gave her the most enormous hug as if he had known her for years. She was shocked and taken aback, but once she had assessed the situation, she smiled and looked indulgently at Sam.

"Do you know?" she said, " I haven't been hugged like that for ages. You can come to my house anytime!" We were most grateful for her good nature and apparent joy at being hugged but realised that our problems were still unfolding. In the meantime, Sam was making his way home in the rain completely unperturbed by what had just happened, happily putting his thumb up at all the passing motorists, just as he'd always done!

Chapter 4

"Ring Julie! Ring Julie?" Sam demanded, then questioned as he stood in the corner of the room holding the phone and looking at me with expectation.

"No, Sam," I said with exhaustion as he asked me for the seventh time whether he could ring his foster mum. Every time he spotted a phone box he'd be in like a shot, pressing all the buttons and pretending to talk to Julie. At first we thought it was funny but keeping tabs on him when we were out was a full time job. We were finding that making allowances for his insecurity, and trying to help him to settle, made disciplining him extra difficult.

"Ignore the bad and praise the good," was the advice we had been given by the child psychiatrist whom we saw once a month. "Allow him to ring his foster mum once a week only, and then you'll have to be firm and say, no more." We'd bought him a toy telephone, we'd tried to distract him but he knew the difference between a toy phone and a real one and it was the real one he was after. The almost obsessive behaviour was beginning to get me down. It was the same with the favourite video that he'd brought with him. How many times during the day are you expected to watch an overgrown cunning tomcat thwack a poor undeserving mouse over the head with a frying pan?

"More!" Sam would demand as the credits rolled up he screen, "More Tom!" At first I had indulged him, thinking that the familiarity was good for him, a link with his past life - providing continuity. Tom and Jerry were alive and kicking, so his relationship with them remained the same. They weren't dead, and this friendship was not going to end brutally. I was going to make sure of that! We watched Tom pound Jerry into the ground with a sledge hammer and I couldn't help noticing that Sam seemed to find the ferocity both stimulating and amusing. Sometimes you just can't win, I thought to myself glumly as I stared out of the window trying to think of how I could distract him and turn the loud flashing, thumping and crashing machine off in the corner.

"The house is too small," I'd complained to John. "We've only one main room for us all to sit in and when the television is on, it completely dominates. We haven't got a separate dining room, it's only a dining area off the lounge and the kitchen isn't even big enough to go and sit in so I can have ten minutes to myself during the day." Already I was beginning to feel the strain. A mum around the corner, or a sister, would have been wonderful to off-load to, and would have given Sam and me a change of scene, especially on wet days. Sam's insecurity was showing itself in many ways, the obsessive behaviour was one, but the other was wanting to hold my hand all the time and take me everywhere with him, like a comforter or an old blanket. He wanted me as a playmate to join in his games, he wanted me to sit next to him at the table, he wanted me to go outside with him and look in the garage for his bike, he wanted me to stay and play when the boys next door came round. He'd stand outside the door when I went to the bathroom calling under the crack in the door. I hadn't watched the news for nearly three weeks and I began to feel I was losing touch with the rest of the world.

Social Services came to my aid with the suggestion of a Family Aid to come and sit with Sam so that I could get out a couple of times a week. She was called Sharon and only lived around the corner. It wasn't until the end of the first session when I was still standing at the lounge door gossiping to Sharon that I realised I'd never actually made it into town, which had been the original plan.It was obvious that I just needed another adult to talk to. So it was decided that from then on Sharon would take Sam round to her house to clean out the fishpond or do some other menial task just to enable me to have friends round or a bit of space to myself.

It was at that time, on one of the few occasions I made it into town, that I decided I needed a boost and so booked into the hairdressers to have a perm. My hair had started to look lack-lustre and had appeared to lose its bounce. I thoroughly enjoyed having someone running around after me for a change, despite having to give the stylist a blow by blow account of life with Sam. After the first wash a few days later, I was forced to return to the salon to point out that my hair was one big flop.

"I can't understand it," mused the stylist, "It's never happened before. Have you been under any kind of strain lately?" It was to be two years before I could get my hair to take another perm.

One of the real pleasures that I had been looking forward to in anticipating the adoption of a small child was indulging myself in the big shops amongst the children's clothes, something that I'd enviously watched other mothers do. On returning from spending my first session there, I was so excited I couldn't wait to show Sam the new stripy blue and white dungarees and matching cream chunky Arran sweater. For once, I thought to myself, I'm going to put my needs before Sam's and enjoy dressing him up.

"Not want those fings, want Sam's fings!" he shouted crossly as he swept the new clothes across the bed in one go. "You have those, want Sam's jumper!" I knew when I was defeated; it seemed obvious that the new clothes threatened his security - his own second-hand clothes and toys brought from foster mum's were a vital part of his identity. If changes were to be made, it was Sam who would dictate the pace, not us. It was to be eighteen months later before I could finally throw away the last piece of second-hand clothing that he had arrived with.

Trying to keep Sam safe was a constant worry especially as we lived on a fairly busy road. I must admit that it wasn't until we got Sam that I began to notice how fast drivers went up and down it. I had wondered about approaching the local council for a sign to be placed near our house saying, "Slow Children Playing," but I thought that Sam might take it personally when he eventually started to read, and so I decided against it! Instead we had to solve the problem of how to keep him off the road, while at the same time allowing him to utilize the large tarmac space at the front which provided a good hard playing area. We couldn't have gates across as the area was too wide and even then they would need to swing out into the road to open, so we solved the problem by parking one of the cars across the bottom of the drive, blocking the spaces either side with stepladders and buckets. It didn't look very pretty but the neighbours understood our reasons and provided we cleared it away at night, were very supportive.

It was on this functional play area that we began to see what a marvellous sense of balance and spatial awareness Sam had. His favourite toy was a Kettler racing car which he pedalled and we would often make a little race track for him using skittles and cones. Needless to say, this attracted the boys from next door and so we would get the stopwatch out and time who could complete the circuit the fastest. Sam was a good two years younger than the youngest boy and we noted with pride his ability to reverse the car round the cones and skittles and into quite small gaps without touching anything.

Bedtimes were also a major source of concern as Sam hated being left by himself, so every night after his story and lights out, books would be thrown from shelves, and toys hurled across the room. Often he would take it upon himself to do a quick tour of the other bedrooms to see what interesting things he could find lying around. If dangerous objects had been moved out of his way to a higher shelf, then he would climb up bookcases to get them and no amount of persuasion would make him give back whatever he had taken. He did not seem able to read situations and sense when we were really cross and had had enough; he seemed to take a great delight in pushing us right to the edge. If we tried to retrieve the dangerous article then it would turn into a steeplechase around the landing - jumping over beds, diving under chairs and behind bookcases. Although we both lost a few pounds, his lack of understanding and temper tantrums remained a problem.

In an effort to help us with a little boy who was making slower progress than originally anticipated, Social Services suggested that many of his tantrums could be due to frustration over not being able to express himself and so Language Therapy once a week was suggested. Although it was a relief to have someone else on board trying to help us, I was concerned about Sam's lack of concentration and discipline causing difficulties in a group situation and wondered how much "sitting nicely" would be involved.

We were met in the reception of the health centre by five or six overfriendly children who looked as though they all belonged to the same extended family. Some had National Health glasses, one had a patch over his eye, the rest had curly hair and runny noses. Sam had never seen a patch over anyone's eye before and stared curiously.

"What dat?" he enquired in a loud voice pointing at the little boy's eye.

"It's an eye patch, to help that little boy's other eye get better," I tried to explain as discreetly as I could.

"Sam want one!" I tried to distract him with a book which was unfortunately a very old copy of Captain Pugwash. My heart sank as Sam's finger expertly picked out a gruesome looking pirate with an eye patch. All the world had an eye patch except Sam.

"Why he got patch?" asked Sam, fascinated.

"Well probably because someone hurt his eye in a fight," I added tentatively.

"He fighting?" asked Sam, full of admiration, pointing at the little boy across the room.

"He's always fightin', that one," a rather large lady on the next chair interjected. Sam slipped off his chair and went to stand next to the boy with the eye patch studying him closely. He looked like someone he wanted to make friends with! When the door of the Speech Therapy room opened he went in quite happily with his new-found friend.

It was about three weeks later, while reading all the notices on the health centre notice board and waiting for Sam's session to end, that a quietly spoken but rather breathless lady came up to me and asked if she could have a word,

"We feel it might be sensible to leave Sam's Speech Therapy sessions for a while," she panted, "We feel that his language gain is incidental and to be honest, he is disrupting the rest of the group. We are having to put a lot of energy into controlling him and just making him sit down. I've just had to chase him round the circle of chairs to try to get him to sit down and to be honest, he thinks it's just a game."

I was shocked, disappointed and embarrassed all at once but understood the problem entirely. "Wait 'til I get him home," I thought angrily, but then my anger quickly disappeared as I looked towards the opening door and saw that the first child out was Sam, wearing an eye patch!

Chapter 5

"Look dad, there's a Virgin!" Several men's heads swivelled round simultaneously in order to view this interesting sight, only to be disappointed to see a bullet-headed train with white stripes on a black and red background swish past on the other side of the river.

"How many carriages did it have?" encouraged John, who had spent the time, between ordering the meal and awaiting its arrival, watching the trains on the other side of the estuary. We had been working on trying to get Sam to notice differences between things using 'spot the difference pictures,' (puzzles with lines of identical symbols) which tricked him because on closer inspection they weren't identical at all. We tried to use anything we could think of when we were out to encourage him to look more carefully and take more notice, instead of dashing around like a hyperactive bluebottle.

"His visual perception is poor," we had been told by the educational psychologist who had been assigned to Sam while he had been in care. "He needs to begin to be able to distinguish between different letter shapes and look for similarities and differences."

It had been a big con to persuade him to come and sit next to us and look at the trains on this gloriously bright June evening. We had to persuade him to get off the enormous brightly painted play galleon thoughtfully provided by the restaurant, over which children were swarming like flies, and tell him his chips were ready, otherwise he wouldn't have come. After five minutes of watching he was still interested and apparently remembering the different liveries. There was obviously hope, but still a lot of catching up to do. Meanwhile there were chips and sausages to be demolished and lots more playing to be done.

Playgroup was in a school room attached to a church in a large west country village. The ladies had been running it for years and were very reassuring when I explained about Sam.

"His last playgroup leader says that he has difficulty sharing, taking turns and sometimes can be aggressive when he can't get his own way. Also," I explained as if talking to his teacher at an open evening, "I'm worried about his painting."

"Oh, he'll get plenty of opportunity for that," the pleasant-faced middle aged lady reassured me, "We have a painting table set out everyday!" she announced with great pride.

"Oh, it's not the opportunity to paint that I'm worried about," I said, "It's the colours he uses."

"They can mix their own!" she announced with great pride, "We put all the primary colours out for them, red, yellow and blue and then we show them how to mix the secondaries, purple, orange and green." You'd have thought that she was telling me that the group had just had an Ofsted inspection and come out with flying colours, her pride was so evident.

"No, I mean it's the predominance of black that worries me," I ventured, "Everything that comes home is black." I recounted the black houses, cars, flowers and people that Julie had kept to show me from his previous playgroup and I noticed her confident stance change to one of indulgence maybe tinged with pity.

"He'll grow out of it," she tried to reassure me, "I think you're worrying needlessly. Go and have a nice cup of tea with the other mums. It'll do you good to talk to them." Those were really the words that I wanted to hear and, moreover, to believe. I didn't think for one minute that the problem was going to be solved as easily as that, nevertheless a cup of tea was always acceptable and so I sidled over to the group of mums at the tea bar.

"He does it every morning without fail." I came in on the tail end of a conversation from a diminutive woman with a red face and fluffy brown hair, "She says he'll grow out of it, but he's been doing it for weeks now and there's no sign." She sighed in exasperation and shook her head in disbelief that she could have raised a child that was so peculiar.

"Don't worry yourself, our Wayne used to borrow my jewellery and strut about looking like the Queen o' Sheba until he was four. There's no point in worryin'," another mum replied, quite pedantically.

I was soon to discover what it was that this mum found so embarrassing about her son, Luke. I noticed a small, dark haired, shy boy walk quietly through the big oak door of the schoolroom and head straight for the dressing-up box. His activity became quite frantic as he searched through the box until he found what he was looking for; a beautiful pink dress with at least three net petticoats and a lacy pink top that looked as if it had come straight out of a fairy story. He proceeded to pull it on over his jeans and tee-shirt without one iota of self consciousness and then proceed to the sand tray as if it was the most natural thing in the world. Meanwhile, his mum was covered in confusion, surrounded by a group of other mums, consoling her and trying to distract her with cups of tea. At least I wasn't the only anxious mother in the group I thought to myself with relief.

My problems were of a different nature, I observed, as I watched Sam grab a big fat wax crayon, holding it as though he was stirring the Christmas pudding, and making large indecipherable scribbles all over the page. After each scribble he threw the paper on the floor and got a new piece. In two minutes he had got through enough paper to fill a phone book and the playgroup leader was looking worried.

"Come and play on the Construction Table," she cajoled in a cheery voice in an effort to distract him. "Let's see what we can make together." Within minutes Sam had been distracted by another child swishing a plastic sword and he was off his chair, all thoughts of making things forgotten, his only intention to liberate the sword at all cost. Within minutes a tussle had begun between Sam and the boy in the pink fairy dress. I was greatly relieved when the playgroup leader announced,

"Circle time everybody, let's see who can carry their chairs nicely and make a big circle."

The last ten minutes of the session consisted of finger rhymes, songs and stories when the children were expected to sit and listen nicely. I knew ten minutes would be far too long for Sam to sustain his interest and concentration and wasn't surprised to see him slipping off his chair after two minutes and trying to hide underneath it. He was hauled back up and deposited firmly back on his seat by a well meaning helper who then proceeded to show him how to manipulate his fingers in time to the music in order to get him back on task. Despite her good intentions he was off his chair again in seconds, swiftly diving under it, only to complete one circuit around the edge of the circle before he could be caught. I knew that Sam preferred this game of chase much more than exercising his fingers and the catching game became an embarrassing feature at the end of every session. One day two boys decided that the catching game looked such good fun that they decided to join in as well, resulting in Sam having to go into the kitchen to "help wash up."

It was about three weeks into the playgroup sessions that I was finally dispatched by the playgroup leader to the village tea room for an hour's time out, after Sam had nearly brought the session to a standstill. She obviously felt awkward admonishing him in front of me, particularly after she'd told me what sterling work she thought I was doing.

It had all started with Sam's great haste to be first at everything, first to take his chair into the circle, first to get his milk and biscuits, first to get his coat on at the end of the session and on this particular sunny day, first to line up at the door in order to get ready to play out in the small garden area on the big toys. This desire to be first apparently emanated from the need to look after himself from a very early age, to make sure that his basic needs were met; now it resulted in inappropriate and often aggressive behaviour. It was this desire to be first at the school room door that had got Sam into trouble for pushing and had resulted in him being sent to the back of the line. His pushing had unsettled some of the other little boys who had then taken it upon themselves to have a go as well and it was a full five minutes before everyone had been nicely spaced out and had stopped wriggling about like a bag of worms! That was when Sam had given one almighty push from the back and the whole line of children had fallen forwards like a pack of dominoes into a chaotic heap on the schoolroom floor! I was grateful to make my escape to a quiet tearoom to recover.

It was almost a relief when the 1992 General Election was forced upon us as I welcomed the change of focus and an 'adult' diversion. It was on the morning when the election results were still being counted that we nearly lost Sam. It was convenient that the kitchen was positioned at the front of the house, thus enabling us to wash up while still observing Sam, which was essential in his case. Having stayed up late the night before to watch the results being counted, and being glued to the television in the early morning to see the overall result, we were in no fit state to supervise a hyperactive four year old. It must have been when John went to the front door, to collect the two pints of milk delivered every morning, that, in his hurry to get back to the screen, he forgot to check that the front door had been securely fastened behind him. Ten minutes later our very red-faced, out-of-breath neighbour from across the road knocked on the door and asked,

"Have you lost anything?" Annoyed at being interrupted while trying to assess the results of the election, I hurriedly answered that we hadn't.

"Think again," she said with a twinkle in her eye.

"Boo!" shouted Sam who was thoroughly enjoying being part of the game. Unable to contain himself any longer, he jumped out from behind her voluminous skirt with bare feet, still wearing his blue and white stripy pyjamas.

"I was washing the breakfast dishes," our neighbour explained with obvious amusement, "when I saw John open the front door to take in the milk. He can't have shut it properly because Sam slipped out about fifteen seconds later. He's been running up and down the street for the last two minutes putting his thumb up at all the cars as they drive past, so I thought you hadn't realised that he was out." It sounded as if she was talking about a pet dog, but I was so shocked at the possible consequences of what she had just described that for a moment I was speechless. "You were having a lovely time weren't you Sam?" she said, smiling at him fondly as she relinquished his hand. He didn't wait to be told off, but just pushed past me into the hall on his way to the dining room to find his breakfast.

"Oh, by the way," my neighbour grinned gleefully as she made her way back down the drive, "Did you know that the Tories are in again?"

For me, the day had definitely not got off to a good start!

Chapter 6

'Improve attention skills, improve social skills with peers, improve ability to stay on task for reasonable periods, improve ability to conform to normal expectations of behaviour.' I had to stop reading the long list of 'improves' before I became overwhelmed by the apparently highhanded demands being made on Sam after only three terms at infant school. His 'Statement' (of Special Educational Needs) had been sent to us for our information and to sign if we were in agreement with the list of objectives to be put into practice for the next academic year. I knew that we would both have reservations about signing this ambitious and bold statement of intent and eventually we agreed to substitute the words 'work towards' for 'improve', setting a much more realistic and sensitive target for a little boy who had undergone so many major upheavals in the first five years of his life.

"Does he have to start school this September?" I had asked the gently-spoken infant teacher who had come to the house to meet Sam one gloriously sunny and hot July afternoon. "He's just not ready," I had implored as she shook her head at me, stating quite categorically that it was the law that all children should start school in the term when they were five.

"We've only had him just over a year and there are so many problems that need sorting out before he goes to school. Couldn't we get a special dispensation or something?" I had asked weakly as I led her through the dark sitting room and out through the patio doors into the brilliant sunshine. It was hard to imagine any problems existing on such a beautiful day, full of hope and promise. I had arranged the garden furniture as informally as possible, two floral pink and green sun loungers with a white wrought iron table set in between, a matching large pink and green umbrella slotting neatly through the hole in the middle of the table. The rockery, small bubbling pebble fountain and brilliant green lawn looked perfect bathed in the afternoon sunshine and the infant teacher sank gratefully down onto her seat, commenting,

"This is a lovely garden. I don't often get treated like this when I go and meet a new pupil!"

On my return, with a tray loaded with tall chinking glasses of juice and ice, I wasn't at all surprised to see Sam on the remaining sun lounger, feet up, tee-shirt off, eyes closed with face tilted up to the sun as if catching the rays on some exclusive beach in St. Tropez. He was responding in the most laid back manner to the questions his teacher was asking him, as if it was the most natural thing in the world to meet your teacher for the first time half dressed while lying prostrate on a sunbed. As our patio was exceptionally small and only allowed for two big seats I had talked Sam through the visit beforehand, suggesting that once he had met his teacher he might like to go inside, watch his favourite video, and have his drink and biscuits in there as a special treat. He had appeared to respond to the idea very well initially, but now no amount of cajoling or persuading could get him to move off the sunbed. Having hit the chocolate biscuits myself recently, I dared not risk the sunbed taking the weight of the two of us, and proceeded to conduct the next ten minutes of the meeting perched like a garden gnome on a very sharp stone at the edge of the rockery. I could imagine the teacher making a mental note for her diary 'weak parenting skills, will need firm boundaries!'

It might have been the look of pain that swept across my face while still balancing on that sharp rock that made the infant teacher suggest that we go inside to finish our conversation, leaving Sam to sunbathe by himself in the garden. Whatever the reason, I was grateful for her tact and expertise in alleviating an embarrassing situation as we made our way back into the darkened sitting room.

She offered lots of helpful ideas about making life easier for Sam at school, such as ensuring that he could dress and undress himself for P.E. and swimming; wearing shoes with velcro fastenings if he couldn't tie his own laces, and wearing trousers with elasticated waists to save the hassle of belts, buckles and zips. Dressing and undressing had never been a problem for Sam - it was something that he could do like lightning - but the finished result often left a lot to be desired! Trousers on inside out, jumpers on back to front, shoes on the wrong feet. Sam didn't seem to notice as there was always too much playing to be done! She was also very reassuring in her final comments as she stood up to go - saying that from what she had seen of Sam so far that afternoon, she didn't envisage he would be in the special unit attached to the school for long, and that once she had completed her assessment of him he would probably be able to transfer to the main part of the school very quickly. I was full of admiration for this quietly spoken, calm, knowledgeable lady who had managed to reassure me in a very short space of time about how Sam's needs would be met within this special unit, despite his social and emotional immaturity and his language delay. She was keen to see Sam before she left, so we slid the patio doors open, blinking out into the brilliant sunshine - only to glance down at a little blonde figure curled up on the sun lounger fast asleep, clutching his ginger bear in one hand and the thumb of the other tucked into his mouth!

The bright red P.E. bag with the draw-string that

granny had made was nearly as big as he was, as the small, blond, blue-eyed boy paused on the step for a photograph, showing the camera his new velcro shoes and grey trousers with the elasticated top. It was a bright September morning and we were both trying to be very positive about Sam's first day at school. He was his normal happy-go-lucky self; despite our frequent games of school in the summer holidays, he clearly had no perception of what school was about or indeed why he was going!

I was concerned that after such a long time Sam might have forgotten his teacher's visit but he was quick to make up for lost time and threw himself against her, giving her the most enormous hug as if he would never let her out of his sight again. She handled him very carefully, firmly prising him away and making him wave "goodbye to mummy", carefully reiterating that he would see again me again that afternoon. I marvelled at her remarkable sensitivity and calmness, knowing how important it was to reassure a child who had been parted from too many people he cared about so often in his young life. The tears that streamed down my face that morning as I walked back to the car were not ones of relief at finally having time to myself for the first time in eighteen months, but of concern for Sam and the demands which I knew would be placed upon him. I was worried about his ability to cope with them at this stage of his life when we, his carers, were still only prospective adoptive parents, both of us at different times having doubts about whether we could cope with such a demanding little boy. So much rested on school and his ability to conform and settle in. We desperately wanted him to make mainstream education and we didn't know if we could cope with him going into a special school, begging the question, did we love him enough?

We had been told by Social Services that all Sam needed was a mum and a dad, consistent boundaries and lots of love and attention. They had told us that the first eighteen months to two years would be the most demanding and difficult but after that we should have a "normal" boy. We sincerely hoped that that would be the case.

"His social behaviour is still giving me cause for concern," Sam's infant teacher informed us as tactfully as she could, after he had been in her class for six months. "His tendency to act impetuously impedes successful integration into a normal mainstream classroom. At the moment I would find it difficult to recommend him for mainstream education." She paused to give us time to assimilate what she had just said. "He has one more term to improve and then we shall have to make our decision," she told us carefully.

"What about the rest of his work?" I asked, trying to hide my disappointment over his behaviour.

"Well, he is showing some gains in his reading and number work." She paused searching for the right words and I wasn't surprised when there came a 'but,' "But I feel he is under-achieving because of his active behaviour and poor concentration. For example, the other day the children had been set the task of writing their names. Some can do it free hand and some, like Sam, are still at the stage where they need to trace over dots on paper to help them remember the shapes of their name. It was a quiet activity specifically designed so that I could hear some children read in the reading corner and change some of the children's reading books ready for the weekend. As soon as I had explained to Sam what I wanted him to do I moved away and started to walk to the library corner. The minute I called a child over to begin reading, Sam's head went up to watch what was going on in the classroom and I had to remind him to stay on task," she said with exasperation. "I thought that he was settled again and was just telling a child to go and find the next book in the scheme when Sam called out, 'I know where that book is, I'll get it for you.' He was off his seat in a flash diving into the book box, book bags flying everywhere. No amount of persuasion would make him go back to his seat and get on. In the end I had to get very cross with him and made him miss his playtime for not doing as he was told. He is, at times, a very strong-willed character but at the same time shows chronic insecurity by having to monitor all the movements inside and outside the classroom. As you know, the school office is situated outside the classroom window and he even waves at the postman every morning as he comes in to deliver the post to the school secretary. Why, I even caught him putting his thumb up the other morning. He can, as you know, be over-familiar at times!"

We both smothered a smile as we imagined the scene but then went on to inform her that we had been told that the hypervigilance had been caused by stress and anxiety in his early years. We were at the same time suppressing thoughts of our own, that having had Sam living with us for the past two years, maybe now we could be partly to blame? We murmured our appreciation for all that she was doing for Sam and informed her of the pleasing progress that he was making at home. His ability to sit and watch a video on his own while we were out of the room was growing evidence that he was slowly becoming more confident and self-assured. We didn't tell her that the video machine itself had been mended at least three times after Sam had tried to set it to record his favourite programme, as he had seen John do so many times, and failed miserably. We thoroughly appreciated what she meant when she talked about Sam being very strong-willed and reluctant to do as he was told!

We were absolutely delighted when ten weeks later we were summoned to school again to be told that although she had some reservations, she was going to recommend Sam for mainstream education with the support of an adult helper for most of the week. We were relieved that he appeared to have made it, but it was with great reluctance that we left the security and infinite wisdom of his first teacher, who had always seemed to know exactly how to handle him. This calm, gentle, unassuming lady had won Sam's affection and ours by providing him with firm, safe boundaries, so important to a child who had never experienced any in his early years. Her ability to know when to challenge and when to keep quiet, when to calm him down quietly by sitting him on a chair, not letting him go until he had complete control of his temper, and when to let him out into the playground to run off pent up energy so that he slept in the car on the way home, never ceased to impress and amaze us. We just hoped that his next teacher would be as experienced, perceptive and sensitive to his needs.

Chapter 7

'HISTORY - This year our main area of study has been Ancient Greece. The children have used a variety of sources to gain knowledge and understanding of life at that time as well as considering the continuity and change that has occurred from past to present.'

I studied the end of term school report and reflected on the second year of Sam's formal education, which had certainly had not been a happy one.

Although the school had tried to reassure us, we had remained extremely sceptical when we had learnt that Sam's first teacher in mainstream education was to be an inexperienced probationary teacher straight from college. Despite the fact that we had been reassured that she had been chosen on merit we remained convinced that the decision had been a financial one, as a more experienced teacher would have stretched the school budget beyond what they felt they could afford. Our only hope was that as Sam had been allocated his own classroom assistant for half the week, his special needs would at least be met fifty percent of the time. We had voiced our concerns to his previous teacher, who was also in charge of children with learning difficulties throughout the school, and she assured us that she would be working very closely with the probationary teacher who already was aware of Sam's needs.

We had both tried to remain optimistic about the appointment, and had ignored Sam's tales in the car on the way home from school each afternoon about who had hit whom in class, and who had been sent to the head for misbehaving. We were just greatly relieved that Sam was an interested observer and not a participant, thanks to his allocated supporter. It became obvious as the term progressed and from the measured and careful way the helper talked about life in the classroom that her role was becoming more and more one of classroom management with the class in general than one of educational support for Sam. I began to make shopping and reading games at home in order to move Sam along gently, as we felt that his helper was not being used for his benefit but to support a teacher who was obviously struggling with managing a class of infants. The final confirmation came when I asked Sam, on the way home from school, what he had done that morning with his helper.

"Didn't see her," he replied as he stared out of the car window.

"Why not?" I asked trying to sound unconcerned, "Was she ill?"

"No, 'cos we're having a Greek restaurant. Can I have some sweets?"

"What do you mean, you are having a Greek restaurant?" I quizzed him, convinced he'd misheard. "Are you sure that you've got it right because you're not very good at listening sometimes?" I'd tentatively suggested. "Remember last week when you told us that the Prime Minister was coming to take assembly on Friday morning and you took your autograph book to school especially so that he could sign his name. When I checked with the school secretary it turned out to be the church minister instead." But Sam had lost interest in my amusing recollection and was busy putting up his thumb at passing motorists.

Anxious to get him back on track I asked, "Are you sure she was making a Greek restaurant? I mean, where was she making it?"

"In the library corner, silly!" he was exasperated now by my apparent stupidity, "And tomorrow we are eating some food in there," he said with a flicker of interest.

"Do you know what the Greeks eat, then?" I asked hoping that he may have listened long enough in class to actually learn something.

"Sausages!" he snapped in contempt at my lack of knowledge and understanding of the Greek culture. "They eat sausages!"

I shifted uneasily in my chair as I sat facing the head teacher." Do you think it would be possible for Sam to be taken out of class sometimes for one-to-one tuition with his helper, somewhere quiet, away from noise and distraction, as we feel that his progress in reading and writing has been a little disappointing so far this year?" I'd ventured as tactfully as I could.

"I have to remind you again that the helper for Sam has been allocated to the school to use as we think fit; it does not necessarily mean that she works with Sam."

"Surely the whole point of his helper is to help him," I stated as calmly as I could. "I'm not suggesting that she works on a one-to-one basis with him all the time, as I know that it is important for him to learn to work in a small group situations as well, but as his reading and writing is so slow to develop, it would seem sensible to use his helper perhaps three times a week to take him out on his own."

"This might happen sometimes but it depends on what the classroom teacher has planned and how she wishes to use the supporter. I cannot guarantee this happening on a regular basis," the headmistress stated quite categorically.

Despite this most unhelpful response I soldiered on, "We are also concerned about this history project, the ancient Greeks. Time is not Sam's strong point, he can't even remember what he did yesterday, let alone project back hundreds of years to another country and culture. He seems to be bored with it and doesn't appear to be getting a lot out of it. Don't you think it would be better to choose a topic that younger children find easier to relate to?"

She sighed, as if implying she was weary of explaining the obvious to nuisance parents, then continued.

"It was a project that took a little bit of help getting off the ground," she said carefully. "We realised that we needed to make it more interactive and so, as we work as a team here, we all pitched in and turned the library corner into a Greek restaurant. Now the children fight to get in there," she announced with great pride.

"Yes, I know, Sam has described it," I answered trying to keep the sarcasm out of my voice.

"I have to remind you that I cannot exclude Sam from any of the National Curriculum subjects, as it is laid down by the government that all children have to have access to a broad and balanced curriculum. The history curriculum categorically states that all children in Key Stage One study events from the recent and more distant past in Britain and the wider world."

"Surely," I interrupted, "There must be some flexibility in that for children such as Sam?"

"I can assure you that Sam is enjoying the project as much as any of the children in the class. He is always one of the first in the restaurant in the morning and his helper was only saying the other day that she felt that he was getting something out of it."

We decided not to pursue the interview any further.

It was during this time, at the end of the school day when collecting Sam, that I became very good at reading the signals. If he was the first one out of the door, it meant that he'd had a reasonable day but they were still glad to get rid of him. If he was somewhere in the middle, they had wanted him out quickly, but he'd been distracted by another child, and if he didn't come out at all, I knew he was in trouble and that those dreaded words, 'Can I see you for a minute?' would soon follow.

It was usually to do with Sam's impetuous behaviour towards other children, for which I would apologise and promise to talk to him about it. However, as his short term memory was so bad, the odds were that he would have forgotten all about it by the next day. Sam wasn't a naturally malicious little boy - in fact one of his most endearing qualities was that he was very affectionate and responded well to praise and encouragement - but as there had never been any consistency or firm boundaries in his early years he had become used to looking after his own needs. Consequently there appeared to be a lot of wrongly learnt behaviour to unpick, hopefully while still maintaining self-esteem; not an easy task!

'Ignore the bad behaviour and praise the good' was easier at home than in a class of twenty six; as children are always so quick to label others, it wasn't long before Sam became the class scapegoat. He would often come home from school with bruises, his shirt torn or in his P.E. shoes because someone had thrown his school shoes over the fence in the playground. On one or two occasions he had returned with a letter from school to say he had been involved in a fight with one of the older boys in Key Stage Two who had apparently decided to 'sort him out' because of some minor disagreement in class with a younger brother or sister.

He clearly wasn't ready for the hurly-burly of school. He had had so much to deal with already in his short life; it would have been sensible to delay the start of his schooling until we had built up a secure firm relationship within the family unit and established the trust that was sadly lacking. It was clear in the early days at school that Sam had no idea what was expected of him and school must have seemed a very challenging and confusing place. Despite this he continued to make steady progress at home and was obviously very fond of John and myself whom he was now calling "mummy" and "daddy." Needless to say I was quite surprised one day to be summoned into the headteacher's room and asked to wait.

"As you know we have not had an easy year with Sam," she began.

I resisted the temptation to say 'I told you so!'

"And we have had a particularly difficult time with him today." she went on. "In fact, it took three members of staff to drag him out from under the picnic table!" she added with a flourish.

"Well, I'm sorry to hear that you have had problems managing him today," I began playing for time while I thought of a suitable response. "I think what I would have done in that situation would have been to leave him and wait for him to come out of his own accord," I said, remembering the previous advice we had been given of 'ignore the bad and praise the good'.

"Well, we can't always do that," she stated in a no-nonsense kind of voice, "But this leads me onto what I really wanted to talk to you about and that is his concentration. We have had a discussion and all the staff who deal with Sam feel quite strongly that his lack of attention in the classroom and his hyperactivity all point to one thing." I knew what she was going to say before she said it. "We think that Sam could have Attention Deficit Hyperactivity Disorder". She paused while I assimilated what she had just said, then went on to justify her supposition. "We have other children in the school displaying similar behaviour who have been diagnosed with ADHD and who take regular medication. Maybe it is something which would be worth checking out?"

We decided that a return visit to the original child psychiatrist would set our minds at rest about the ADHD issue, but were informed that, as it had been such a long time since our last appointment, and as we lived outside his area, we would have to use a more local service. We were offered a speedy referral however and managed to get an appointment quite quickly.

At our first session we were asked if we would like Sam to work with a young registrar doctor who would engage him in play therapy while we talked to the child psychiatrist. We were all for this, as an hour to indulge ourselves and offload all our concerns about Sam without the fear of seeming obsessive - and with N.H.S. tea and biscuits thrown in - appealed to our own growing need to be nurtured.

On collecting Sam from the adjoining room at the end of the first session he ran towards us waving a black swirl on a piece of paper that, he informed us, was his house and his mummy and daddy.

"Why don't you use some nice bright colours to paint with?" John had suggested when he saw another dark swirl.

"Not want to, like black best!" he replied most definitely.

"We're a bit concerned about some of his play," the registrar informed us after several sessions. "There seems to be a lot of anger and I think that there are quite a lot of unresolved issues for him. He would benefit from regular play therapy, in fact we have a colleague who runs a group here every Wednesday."

"That's great," I interjected, "I'll bring him along."

"I'm afraid it's not that simple, you see there's a two year waiting list."

"How much would it cost to pay privately?" I asked, undaunted.

"Well, once you start this kind of treatment it usually means a long-term commitment," she began hesitantly. "When we talk about long-term commitment we're talking in terms of two years and this kind of treatment doesn't come cheap. I think Sam would benefit from work on a one to one basis at first, then work in a group situation later." She then proceeded to give me the cost per hour, at which I visibly blanched, choked on my tea and muttered,

"We'll have to think about it, I didn't realise it would be quite as much as that. It would be cheaper to repay the national debt!" Then, as an afterthought, " For the time being he might have to make do with the crêche at the local supermarket!"

"From what you have told me, it would appear that Sam probably hasn't got ADHD but to be certain we could try him on Ritalin. If he has it, you will see an instant improvement." The child psychiatrist was already writing out the prescription as he spoke. "We may have to adjust the dose, each person is different and it might take a while to get it right." John and I looked at each other. This was something we had previously discussed and agreed that we would try to avoid at all costs. We had read the reports and felt that not enough research had been done into the side effects of this particular drug. However, it looked as if we were going to have to use it, if only to diagnose the problem definitively. With the prescription in my handbag, and instructions to collect the drug from the local hospital, we set off for home with very mixed feelings.

It was a while before I plucked up the courage to use the drug and I decided to use it for the Sunday School Nativity Play where Sam had a walk-on, sit-down and do-nothing part. He was the shepherds' helper. It was his job to round up and count the herd of sheep who were played by the youngest children attending Sunday School, who would be wearing sheep masks and dressed in white bobbly material. I felt that as this was his first public appearance it was important that it should go well and he should sit still and remember what to do. I read the prescription carefully and half a tablet at breakfast was carefully given just before we set off for church.

On arrival Sam was taken into the "Shepherds' Room" and transformed into one quite quickly. At this point I was urged by his Sunday School teacher to find my seat in the audience as he had to join the others backstage. With final warnings to behave and 'do it nicely' I slipped into the hall, full of fear and trepidation at Sam's first public appearance. I tried to concentrate on the angel visiting Mary piece, and the donkey ride to Bethlehem, but in the back of my mind I was worrying about Sam's complete lack of awareness about what was expected of him and wondered if he would use his first public performance as an opportunity to show off.

'While shepherds watch their flocks by night' was sung and then three shepherds shuffled onto the stage looking behind them in an expectant manner as if waiting for something to happen. I heard an urgent stage whisper of, "Sam, go on, it's your turn!"

Quite uncharacteristically Sam shuffled on, head down, stopped as if seeming to remember something, then turned slowly around and beckoned something onto the stage, like a bored traffic policeman at the end of his shift. On waddled the sheep,who proceeded to file slowly past Sam to lots of "oohs" and "aahs" from the audience. Following the example of the rest of the shepherds, he then flopped quickly down onto the floor around a pretend camp fire. Even when the angel Gabriel appeared in the sky he didn't look up. Even when the other shepherds shielded their eyes from the glare of this special messenger Sam didn't look up. Even when other nearest shepherd dug him in the ribs, he didn't look up.

"He's gone to sleep," I heard someone behind me snigger, "It must have been counting all those sheep!" More like that blessed Ritalin, I thought to myself grimly.

"We'll have to modify the dose," the child psychiatrist said, quite unperturbed by what I had just told him. "We'll get it right eventually, but it might take some time." We nodded, not completely convinced.

"It could be that as it is making him so sleepy we need to reduce the dosage but you do say there has been an improvement in his concentration?"

"Yes," I agreed, "He certainly seems to be able to stay on task a little better than before."

"I am still not able to say definitely whether it is ADHD or not, "he continued, "but as Sam seems to be benefiting, let's try him on it for say, four weeks and then perhaps review the situation again. I know that both of you are still not happy about using it."

"We're having a few problems with the school at the moment," I ventured, unsure of what his reaction would be to what I was about to ask him next. "We have Sam's Annual Review coming up next week and we wondered whether you would be able to be present to explain in person what you feel about him?"

"If you let me have the date, I'll ask my secretary to look in my diary to see if I'm free," he said without any hesitation at all.

"Thank you," I said pleased that we would have another professional person on our side when it came to assessing Sam's progress and drawing up realistic expectations for the following year. "The school seem convinced that he has definitely got ADHD and it would obviously make their life easier if we put him on permanent medication."

"All I will be able to say to them, is what I said to you earlier, which is he might not have it because the medication does tend to make him sleepy which could be a sign that he doesn't have this condition," he patiently explained.

The day of the Annual Review dawned and we set off to the meeting at the school feeling reasonably hopeful, given the support of a child psychiatrist and the educational psychologist who had also promised to try and be there. Both continued to be optimistic about Sam's progress and felt that, with the right kind of sensitive intervention, he should continue to make progress. Although we had set off in plenty of time we were surprised to see the child psychiatrist's car already in the school car park.

"Gosh, he's keen," commented John, "He's nearly twenty minutes early. That's great, the quicker we can get started the better. Let's go and do battle!" he grinned. "Don't look so serious," he said to me, "It might not be that bad after all."

The school secretary met us in the entrance hall with the words, "They're not ready for you yet, would you like a cup of tea while you wait?" Then she added, almost as an afterthought, "Did you know that Sam's educational psychologist has rung in to say she can't make the meeting today? But she popped in the other day to watch him in the class and has sent this report to be read out at the meeting. Was that tea for two or not?" she asked, almost in the same breath.

"We'll leave the tea, thank you," said John.

"That's a real blow," I whispered to John, "She was our closest ally. She is good at trying to persuade the school to be a little more flexible in their approach to Sam."

"She's probably had to go to court," mused John. One of the drawbacks of our educational psychologist was that she worked for Social Services rather than the Education Department but had agreed to keep Sam 'on her books' as she had known him since a toddler. She felt that continuity for him was important and the fact that she would often require him to do little tests and exercises, to enable her to assess his needs correctly, meant that she had had the opportunity to build up his trust. We had been most grateful over the years for her encouragement, honesty and support.

"I'm supposed to give you this to read while you're waiting," the secretary said, waving in our faces two pieces of A4 paper stapled together in the corner.

"They're ready for you now," we were told as we were led into the headmistress's cramped study to find two empty chairs facing a line of chairs already filled with teachers and our child psychiatrist. We both felt as if we were going to be interviewed for a job in the school! The meeting got off to a brisk pace with the headmistress taking the chair. There was a definite agenda which had to be adhered to, and twice I was told, when I tried to raise a point, that there would be time in the meeting later to talk about that particular issue. The atmosphere in the room seemed intimidating, unsupportive and cold.

"Can I just raise this issue mentioned in the educational psychologist's report?" I asked at the appropriate time in the meeting. "She states that as Sam is still very emotionally immature for his age it would be appropriate to allow him to go into the reception class to take advantage of the sand and water play there. He would be able to play at a much younger level and make up for a lot of the time he lost in his early years," I ventured, hopefully sounding persuasive enough.

"I think that might be difficult to arrange," came the frosty reply, "It is already a large reception class in a small space and Sam can be..." she searched for the most diplomatic word, "... controlling at times. The younger children may find him intimidating."

"But surely, that is the point of having a helper so that she can go with him and make sure that things are running smoothly?" questioned John, who had already sat through forty five minutes of quite a difficult meeting without losing his temper.

"We also have to think about his self-esteem" she said. "He might not like going into a younger classroom."

"Well, that would depend on how it was handled," I interjected, equally as frostily. It was becoming more and more clear as the meeting progressed that there was a hidden agenda. Sam was being portrayed as a problem child who would not fit in to the school's way of working - and that was clearly our problem, not theirs.

"If he was asked to go down to the reception class to help with the sand and water play, I'm sure that would appeal to him enormously," I declared, trying not to sound patronising in any way. "He loves to help and I'm sure he would really enjoy it. Surely you could be flexible enough to accommodate that?" I finished abruptly, feeling that I had been diplomatic enough, my temper coming to the surface in one almighty rush. I suddenly felt angry that we were not being supported and that we should be put in this position after spending the last two years of our lives trying to help a little boy get his life back on track. I felt that it was totally unacceptable that the only 'help' we were getting from his school was inflexibility and coldness.

"Well, perhaps this isn't the right school for Sam?" the headmistress said, appearing to play her final card. Quite clearly it was easier to get rid of a problem than address it, and this was her solution. We needed reinforcements. John turned to the child psychiatrist, who had been remarkably quiet during the whole interview, in the hope that he would interject some positive note into the proceedings.

"What do you think about Sam?" he asked him, "Do you see permanent medication as the only way forward?"

He weighed his words carefully and sighed, "It appears from what I have been told before the meeting commenced and from what has been said in the meeting today that that is the case." We felt completely deserted as if our final ally had suddenly decided to change sides without telling us. We felt defeated. The meeting then came to an informal end and the conversation slid with apparent great relief into other aspects of school life and our son seemed to be forgotten.

The journey home in the car was completed in silence as we both reflected on the outcome of the meeting. Finally John spoke, "We have no choice but to move him. They seem unable to cope with him and are unwilling to be flexible." In view of the recent and unfavourable Ofsted report we had both pored over the previous week, which highlighted 'serious weaknessses', we realised that a move was going to be inevitable. "I think we are going to have to uproot the poor little chap again. More changes, Sam. Sorry, mate!" John added ruefully as we turned into the drive.

Chapter 8

The quietly spoken, fair-haired man leaned back against the arm of the settee, trying to look as unobtrusive as possible as I tried to play with Sam as unselfconsciously as I could. Sam, sensing something unusual was happening, went into hyperactive mode, a device I often thought he used to prevent anyone getting too close for comfort, and proceeded to dash from the hall into the lounge and back again, possibly suspecting that this observation heralded yet another move.

"How much liquid does he drink a day?" the homeopath enquired sensitively.

"I couldn't really say," I admitted, feeling very unobservant and grossly inadequate.

"Well," he said patiently, "Does he drink a lot or not much at all?"

"Not much at all," I replied, relieved to be able to answer a question correctly.

"What about eating? Are there any foods that he will not eat?"

"Tomatoes," I answered instantly, pleased at not being caught out again.

"Interesting," he mused as he scribbled down my responses.

"Yes, I really do think that I will be able to help Sam," he volunteered quietly at the end of the hour's home visit, for which I had paid a very reasonable sum. "You see, the beauty of homeopathy is that it either works or it doesn't," he added. "After the body has rebalanced itself there aren't usually any side effects at all. I think that I will be able to make up a prescription for Sam that will help with his concentration and will generally calm him down."

"That is tremendous," I gushed with relief. "We

really didn't want to have to use Ritalin but feel that as he is starting a new school, we want to give him the best start we can. In a strange situation we always notice that the hyperactivity gets worse and would seem to directly mirror his anxiety."

He smiled, seeming to understand without me having to say any more. "I shall send you the prescription through the post. It will be in an envelope with correct dosages to take, but I want you to ring me at home, as soon as he has taken the first tablet, so that we can fine tune the dosage and get it just right for Sam." What a relief, I thought as I let the homeopath out of the door. Here was someone who genuinely understood our predicament and was unobtrusively helpful and positive; just what we needed at that moment.

"Of course we will be able to help Sam," the headmaster had stated over the phone the week before when we had rung the mainstream school to enquire about places. "Why not bring him along for a look around to see what you think and more importantly, what Sam thinks?" We liked the way the child's needs appeared to be put first, even over and above those of the parents, which is the way it should be. We both felt that maybe our luck was changing and that we had finally found a school which would be able to cater for him.

The headmaster was ready for us when the school secretary showed us to seats in the bright attractive entrance hall and came striding out of his office, arm extended ready to shake hands, not with us, but with Sam. Sam, thoroughly enjoying the attention and being treated as an equal, grinned and extended his hand, nearly shaking the headmaster's hand off with delight and enthusiasm. We were then treated to a full tour of the school where we were able to take in the bright, stimulating wall displays, see the children busily engaged in their activities and notice the underlying buzz of enthusiasm that seemed to permeate the atmosphere. We were introduced to the enthusiastic teacher whose class Sam would be joining and given the opportunity to look into her classroom and observe the children at work. There were lots of practical activities going on, which involved the children moving around the room and interacting with each other. I could tell that Sam was really interested .

We made our way back to the headmaster's room to finalise things. No time was wasted in addressing all questions to Sam.

"What's your favourite book?" the headmaster asked him. That might stump him, I thought to myself. I decided to help him out without appearing to seem too pushy.

"It doesn't have to be one that you have read yourself, it could be one that someone has read to you," I offered as a prompt. That was all he needed,

"Danny the Champion of the World!" Sam replied without hesitation.

"Ah, that's a good book. I like that one too," the headmaster said reassuringly. "Do you know who wrote it?"

Oh no, a trick question, I panicked, but before I could think of a response Sam had replied,

"Roald Dahl." My heart swelled with pride. Wow! I thought to myself, he does listen and he can remember things when he's interested.

"Well done for remembering that," John interjected, equally impressed.

"Have you read that book yourself, Sam, or has someone read it to you?" the headmaster enquired, still addressing his comments to Sam.

"Dad reads it to me at bedtime," he responded quite happily, not realising the importance of his responses. The headmaster was quite clearly assessing us all as we walked along the light airy corridors back to his office. "I like stories," Sam volunteered almost on cue. He couldn't have behaved better. I glanced across at John who gave me a reassuring wink.

"Any questions you would like to ask?" the headmaster enquired pleasantly.

"Because of Sam's poor start in his early years, he has missed out on vital play experiences," I began hesitantly. "According to the most recent educational psychologist's report he still needs time to consolidate these. Do you think it would be possible for him to go to the Infants', maybe in the context of 'helping' to enable him to catch up?" I enquired praying that he would be flexible enough to say yes.

"I don't see a problem with that," he replied instantly, "We've applied to the Authority to make his statement up to 0.8, so that he'll get an adult helper for 80% of the time. I'm sure the Reception class would welcome an extra pair of hands!"

"Thank you so much," we both replied instantaneously.

"You're very welcome - and we shall look forward to seeing Sam next term," he said, shaking our hands warmly as we made our way to the door. There were tears in my eyes as we walked down the school drive swinging a very contented little boy between the two of us.

It became obvious during the first two or three terms in Sam's new school that his social and emotional development were the main focus of the school's attention; together with that of building his self esteem.

His enthusiasm when being collected at the

school gate was evident, and he was often full of all the interesting things which he had been doing.

"Guess what?" he demanded on the second week of term as I drove him home from school. "We've been shopping and baking today!"

"Wow, that sounds a lovely thing to do at school" I enthused. "Tell me more."

"First we had to go to the secretary for some pretty cash," he declared with great importance.

"I think you mean petty cash!" I corrected him, trying to hide my amusement. "Go on," I encouraged.

"Then we had to walk into the village to buy the things from the shops."

"What did you buy?" I asked.

"We had to get eggs and flour and sugar and ..." he squeezed up his eyes in an effort to remember.

"Margarine?" I volunteered.

"Yes! That's it!" shouted Sam obviously impressed. "Then we had to go back and wash our hands and tie each others' pinafores and then we could start.

"What did you do first?" I asked, knowing full well how important it was for Sam to remember the correct sequence of events.

"We-e-ll," he started, obviously playing for time, trying to mask his difficulty in remembering. "I think we had to go and get those weighing things. I can't remember what they 're called," he said, obviously searching for the correct word deep in the recesses of his brain.

"Scales, weighing scales," I volunteered.

"That's it!" declared Sam with obvious admiration, and I could tell that at that moment I had gone up in his estimation. He looked at me in the rear view mirror as if seeing me for the first time as a person and not just a provider of clean clothes and hot food.

"You could come into school to help if you want, like

Jessica's mum," he encouraged me as if awarding me great prize.

"I might just do that," I replied, pleased he wanted me to share the pleasures in his life. As I answered, I experienced a real tingle of joy. For the first time in our relationship, I felt Sam had offered a genuine hand of friendship born out of respect, admiration and, dared I hope, trust? I decided to leave the interrogation about the baking as I felt that what we had just achieved was more important than remembering how to bake buns.

And so it continued: the excitement over the special job in assembly when Sam had to place the acetate sheets on the overhead projector for the whole school during the hymn singing, the clever arrangement whereby there was always someone there to "catch him" if he went wrong, as he did during the Harvest Festival Service - resulting in the whole school singing verses one and two through twice while the music teacher frantically tried to catch Sam's attention to remind him to switch the sheets. "We needed the extra practice anyway!" was the headmastermaster's response by way of explanation to the audience.

The sense of importance as Sam was asked to go in extra early to help the school caretaker put out the chairs for the summer term music concert; the way he was asked to be a stage hand and move the scenery at the Christmas production - all this helped to provide Sam with a sense of self worth and achievement which was urgently needed. It was with great joy that we opened his first report at the end of his first year at his new school and read the following words, "Sam displays a happy, positive attitude in and around school and he is always willing to help others."

It was during the following school year that Sam's new-found confidence began to display itself by wanting to participate in the many and varied after-school activities on offer.

"Can I stop for Gym Club as well, mum?" he asked brightly one morning while chewing his cornflakes.

"Well, don't you think it might be good for Dad to do something on his own?" I teased, knowing full well that he was desperate to go because John had offered to help out, and he was wanting to show off his dad to the other children.

"No, I can help him," he'd responded in all seriousness. That was what we were worried about. Would he exploit the situation and not do as he was told? Would it end up being embarrassing for John? It was something John was going to have to find out, so with dire warnings on the morning of the club about what would happen if he wasn't a good boy, I waited anxiously at home for John's report.

"I was really proud of him," he said later that evening. "He was the first to open the door into the hall, the first to get the light on in the cupboard, the first to wheel the trolley out and start to place the mats across the hall floor. He was desperate to impress me with how competent he was. I think he wanted to make me proud of him. It was quite moving really," he added quietly. We both went quiet as we remembered the unnecessary warnings which had been issued that morning.

"I really do think that the homeopathy is helping him," I volunteered. "He seems to be more aware of what is expected of him. I think he is maturing, albeit slowly but I think we are witnessing some changes."

"He was great in the lesson as well," said John enthusiastically. "He has a good sense of balance and can do handstands, cartwheels and vault over the box. He's not tentative or shy like some of the children, he's willing to have a go at most of the challenges I set them."

"Great," I replied, " That's Gym Club sorted then, at least we've found something that he can shine in," I said with relief.

Unfortunately this wasn't the case on the football field. "He just doesn't understand the game," John would say despairingly as he related the after-school football practice to me, kick by kick, over a cup of tea in the kitchen after depositing Sam in front of the television. "It's just so embarrassing!" he admitted somewhat guiltily.

"Well, who does understand football?" I volunteered in Sam's defence.

"He made a blinding save," continued John as if he hadn't heard me, "And then, instead of kicking or throwing it straight out again, he put it down on the ground, walking back to the goal line just as the opposing centre forward ran in to take advantage and shoot at an empty goal! Fortunately Sam managed to kick it out just in time but the rest of his team mates were shouting, "Sam, what *are* you doing?" It was obvious from John's expression as he was speaking that he was reliving every painful moment. "It's such a shame," he continued, "As he desperately wants to play in the school team and he's never missed a practice!"

"Never mind," I said trying to console him, perhaps they'll play him in the 'B' Team, even if it is only for ten minutes."

Unfortunately this was never to materialize despite the promises which Sam assured us had been made by the team coach. "I'm thinking of playing him in the next match," the coach had said to John when Sam had come home from yet another practice in tears because he hadn't been picked.

"I realise the problem," John had said, "But do you think that you could play him just once in the 'B' Team? Could you play him mid-field do you think, just to say he's had a game?" He tried to persuade him, but it never happened. It seemed to be a win-at-all-costs policy, and the coach didn't appear to want to take the risk of playing Sam at all.

It was at this time that John decided he needed some light relief, and to witness some real football action, so he booked a ticket to see Derby County, his favourite club of many years' standing, play at Hillsborough in Sheffield.

"I've booked my ticket," he informed me one evening, "I'm really looking forward to it. It should be a really good game. I'm going up on the train, I've booked a first class seat, I might even treat myself to lunch."

"Have you got me a ticket?" Sam asked, caught up in the excitement of planning a trip.

"We-e-ll. ... No," said John. "I thought I'd go on my own this time."

"But I want to come too!" he cried. "I want to watch Derby win as well!"

He was clearly most upset at not being included in this exciting expedition.

"I didn't think that you were interested enough to sit through a whole game," John came back at him, by way of defence. "Anyway," he added decisively, "I've got my ticket now!"

And so it was, that two weeks later, I stood on the station platform and waved them both off looking like liquorice allsorts in their black and white hats and scarves.

"I haven't managed to book another seat next to

mine," John had informed me after he had relented and bought a second ticket for the match for Sam, "But I'll try to get someone to swap seats when I get to the ground." Sam had been delighted by the change of heart and had been looking forward to the trip for weeks. John wasn't so sure. He had been looking forward to reading his paper from front to back, something he never seemed to achieve since we'd had Sam. He had even bought himself a new CD in anticipation of the luxurious isolation the long train journey would provide.

"You'll be a good boy for dad?" I reminded him as I'd stuffed his bag full of small games and story tapes to keep him amused.

"Of course I will," he replied, with disgust at my low opinion of his behaviour.

"Well, you can be very tiring sometimes, especially when you chatter away all the time," I tried to remind him.

"I know, I know," he answered without really listening to a word I was saying.

"Just remember that Dad was going for a rest, that's all," I added, wasting my breath.

"Did you manage to change seats with someone when you got to the ground?" I enquired over the phone later that day when they rang from the station platform on their way home.

"No," said John in a weary kind of voice, "I didn't."

"What!" I screeched down the phone, "You mean you let him sit by himself in a crowded football stadium for over an hour? He could have been sat next to anyone!"

"I tried, I really did," explained John. "But it meant splitting two brothers up who go to the game and have the same seats every week, or two families of four who clearly wanted to be together."

"How far away from you was he?" I asked, in disbelief, unable to accept that John couldn't have negotiated harder than he appeared to have done.

"He was only on the row in front, ten seats along to my right," he tried to reassure me. "If you really want to know, I was so busy checking that he was alright and sitting on his seat properly, that I missed the first goal!" he said, with obvious exasperation. "After the first ten minutes he was off his seat and running up and down the steps at the side with another little boy. He wasn't really interested. I had to squeeze past everyone and go and tell him to sit down or else! And that's when I missed the second goal!"

"Then, he went and sat down and appeared to be talking to the man on his right, nineteen to the dozen, you know how he tends to rattle on, usually about nothing? Well, that's when I missed the third goal! I was trying to catch his attention and signal to him to let the man watch the match and be quiet!"

"Oh dear," I tried to sound sympathetic, while suppressing the humour creeping into my voice.

"And that's not all," he continued, "One of the two brothers I was sitting next to, got so fed up with my agitated state that he shouted at me."

"What did he say?" I asked caught up with the drama of the story.

" 'What's up wi' thee lad? You're rushin' around like a bluebottle wi' its bum on fire. Sit thi'sen down. 'E'll be a'reet. You'll give thi'sen an 'eart attack.' "

"He wasn't into plain speaking then?" I said sarcastically, trying to make light of what had obviously been quite a difficult afternoon.

"At half time," John continued like a man in therapy desperate to offload some traumatic event, "I went to see Sam to ask if he wanted a drink or a hot dog. When I got there, he was already munching through a massive bag of sweets, you know, the sort we never let him have because of all the additives. "Where did you get those from?" I asked him.

Before he had time to answer the man next to him butted in and said, "I bought 'em for 'im, mate. I'll try owt to shut the little ****** up!"

At that point John's voice was blotted out by the station tannoy announcing the arrival of the next train. When our conversation resumed again I said,

"I didn't quite catch what the man said, but I assume it was rude?"

"You've got it!" said John. "I thought we ought to change places after that, and so we switched over. I thought I'd stop and talk to Sam until the second half started but do you know what he said to me?"

"No," I replied thinking that it couldn't get much worse.

"Go away, Dad, I don't need you now. I can manage by myself!"

Much later that evening, as I was tucking Sam up in bed, I asked him if he had enjoyed his day.

"It was great," he replied with obvious enthusiasm.

"Did you learn a bit more about football?" I asked him.

"No," he replied, "Not really, but I learned lots more new swear words!"

"I've joined a new club, mum," said Sam one day as we drove home in the car.

"What's that, then?" I asked as I tried to concentrate on the traffic.

"Netball," he said in a very matter of fact kind of voice.

"Netball!" I exclaimed in surprise as I slammed on the brakes, narrowly missing the car in front. "Netball, are you sure?" I asked again, trying to keep the concern out of my voice.

"Yeh, and I'm really good at it because I'm tall," he added as if repeating word for word the team coach's encouraging remarks.

"Are there any more boys in the team then? " I asked, trying not to sound too concerned that I appeared to be stuck with the Billy Elliot of netball.

"No, I'm the only one!" he declared proudly without a trace of self-consciousness, and so we left it at that. Week after week he went enthusiastically to the practices, without a trace of embarrassment about being the only boy, and was a real asset to the team, but never played in a match. It appeared to be girls versus girls in the inter-school netball matches and boys versus boys in the inter-school football matches, so for one reason or another Sam never got a game. Nevertheless, he had a great time on the way home from the practices, as he informed me one day over tea.

"I had really good fun in the graveyard today, Mum," he said, gobbling down fish fingers and peas.

"Really!" I said, wondering what on earth was coming next, "I crouched down behind a grave stone and got the centre and goal attack a direct hit with my water pistol. It was ace! I shouted, 'Two - Nil, Two - Nil,' and then ran off before they could get me!" He was obviously getting a lot more out of school than we had originally imagined!

Chapter 9

"Help me, Mum, don't go!" the plaintive cry came quietly from Sam's lips as I attempted to sidle out of the cinema doors. It was hard to reconcile this with the person who, an hour ago, had been awkward and stroppy, and had refused to cooperate when attempting the twenty-minute work period we insisted upon each day of the school holidays.

"Help me, I don't know if I've got enough money!" He tried to whisper so that his newly acquired friend wouldn't hear and learn the full extent of his difficulties over handling money.

"Well, read the sign," I'd hissed back, frustrated at his unwillingness to have a go.

"What does it say on the card?" I was determined that despite his obvious embarrassment I wasn't going to do it for him, "Go on, read it," I'd encouraged him.

"Regular, one pound sixty." he stammered out. "Medium, one pound ninety. Large, two pounds fifty!" he exclaimed, relieved at being able to get it over and done with.

"Well?" I enquired , "Which one can you afford?"

"Just tell me, Mum," Sam hissed in panic and exasperation as he saw his friend disappear up the stairs to Screen Two. "It'll start without me!"

"No, it won't, you've got plenty of time yet. Look at your money," I said calmly, trying to take the panic out of the situation. " You had five pounds and ten pence when you came in and the ticket cost three pounds fifty, so how much change have you got left?"

Sam looked down at the coins in his hand.

"One pound fifty and ten is......" he wavered and glanced up at a noisy group of teenagers that had just come in the door, all concentration gone. I realised that I was going to have to put him out of his misery.

"OK." I relented, "It's the small carton, isn't it? You've got one pound sixty left. Can you see now why we try to do a little maths every day?" I said, not able to resist a little dig.

"Yes, yes," he replied with bored resignation, "Don't keep going on, Mum," and with that he disappeared up the steps to Screen Two to an important appointment with *The Men in Black*.

We had noticed that even though apparently quite settled in his new school, progress in reading and writing was depressingly slow. The twenty minutes reading practice every night was like trying to climb the steepest mountain in the world without the correct equipment and Sam would approach each reading session with exactly the same words, "Do we have to? How much have I got to read? Can I stop when I get to the bottom of this page?"

There was clearly little or no enjoyment derived from his reading at all, apart from the occasional cursory glance at the picture, often resulting in a long laborious explanation about what he thought would happen next. This was used purely as a delaying tactic, to put off the dreaded reading session. Despite having spent ages trying to help him learn the most commonly occurring words in the English language, he still reversed his letters and constantly read 'was' when he meant 'saw', read 'then' when he meant 'they', and no amount of looking and remembering or playing word games seemed to enable him to commit these essential words to memory.

"We've got it!" I'd triumphantly declared to John after a night playing Snakes and Ladders, when we had substituted these annoying little words to generate the score instead of a dice.

"He's spelled them all correctly!" I'd exclaimed in triumph.

"Well done!" John dug deep into his pocket pulling out a pound coin and handing it to Sam. "It's taken some doing but we've got there in the end!"

It was two days later while playing the same game, that John hissed to me as I passed by the dining room table, "I think I'll ask for a refund! We've forgotten them again!" and sure enough there was Sam struggling to spell 'they'. It was obvious that Sam had problems with his short term memory and remembering things was going to be difficult for him. When listening to him read, John and I found it so frustrating when encouraging him to break a word down into its separate sounds or syllables, for by the time he got to the last syllable he would have forgotten the first one, and so blending them all together would become impossible for him. He would become physically exhausted after reading a page of a book, having to put far more effort and energy into it than you would normally expect; the mechanics of breaking the words down completely absorbing him so that by the end of the page he would still have no idea about what he had just read.

"It's like being stoned to death with marshmallows!" said John, one Sunday evening, after hearing Sam read for twenty minutes, but despite this we still managed to sustain his interest in books by doing a trade-off.

"If you read to me for ten minutes, then I'll read to you for twenty," I had promised him, "Any book you like!" This had succeeded as an incentive and resulted in very long bedtime stories most evenings. On the nights when we were both just too tired, we discovered that story tapes were just as good and helped to stem the insecurity that often returned at bedtime when Sam was alone.

Times tables were a nightmare; we'd try tapes to sing along to, innovative worksheets and all manner of games but it was no good, they just wouldn't stick. Time was also a problem - yesterday, tomorrow, last week, days of the week, months of the year were all beyond Sam's comprehension.

He'd try to explain by long painfully drawn out statements. "Not the day that's just gone, but the day before that one," would often precede an explanation about something. John and I would try and give him enough time to seek out the appropriate word, while at the same time assessing when to help him out to prevent him losing interest.

Writing was also a problem, and the formation and sizing of letters were explained over and over again. Special handwriting paper with more lines than Clapham Junction was bought to help but once transferred onto 'normal' writing paper all was forgotten and he went back to the normal spidery scrawl with constant reminders to leave finger spaces.

Birthdays were a good excuse to get Sam to write *Thank You* letters but somehow he always managed wriggle out of it by using the phone - it was quicker and easier, and anyway, what was all the fuss about?

Jobs around the house were vital as Sam's practical abilities made up for his problems in other areas. Setting the table for dinner was listed as one of these, which was when we noticed that the knives and forks were back to front, upside down and anyway but the right way. The word 'Dyslexia' kept cropping up and we felt that it needed investigating.

"Yes, he could be," volunteered the educational psychologist. "We haven't been able to run any kind of test for that sort of thing because he wouldn't allow us to get too close, metaphorically speaking. He'd use avoidance strategies so that we couldn't pin him down. We've been so busy sorting out his social and emotional behaviour that really we're only just beginning to tackle the educational side of things. We don't really need to run a battery of tests. We know he is experiencing problems with his literacy, so why not try to get him some extra help from a really good primary school teacher offering private tuition?"

And so began the quest to find such a person. We followed up adverts in magazines and local papers but not many teachers offered dyslexia specialisms. We found one who did, but admitted to seeing nearly thirty children a week. We didn't feel that she could possibly give Sam the individual attention which he would need. Besides this, the only gap during her hectic week was 5 o'clock on a Wednesday evening, when Sam had experienced a full day at school and we would have had to fight our way through rush hour traffic into a busy city centre. It was with great relief that we finally found a specialist teacher who was working part-time in a school but who took on a few pupils on Saturday morning, and, yes, she did have just one vacancy for ten thirty. She was also a fully trained counsellor so with the combination of all these skills we felt that divine providence had sent her to us. We signed up straight away and began to enjoy our long but beautiful drive into the countryside each Saturday morning when, after depositing Sam for his lesson, we would enjoy a country ramble, a welcome cup of coffee and a chance to catch our breath while someone else was stoned to death with marshmallows!

Chapter 10

As I dragged the awkward aluminium ladder up the stairs I couldn't help marvelling at the fact that he actually thought the waistcoat would still fit. After all these years Sam's sense of time, and the passing of it, hadn't got any better and the realisation that he had grown hadn't really occurred to him. "It's called 'North meets South' and will you both come and watch me do it? It's on Monday morning." It was hardly the most convenient time of the week for us both to disengage ourselves from work commitments, but the fact that we both now worked part-time had made our respective employers more flexible and sympathetic. We also knew how important it was to support Sam at this particularly vulnerable time in his schooling when he had failed to make mainstream secondary education. Despite the sterling work undertaken by his previous school there appeared to be too much ground to make up and together with Sam's steady but slow progress, this decision was thought to be the best for Sam, with a view to possibly moving him into mainstream, if we felt he could cope with it at a later date.

Sam dragged down the old bit of carpet to place underneath the feet of the ladder to stop it making too great an impression on the landing carpet. I watched him, amazed that he couldn't spell the word *ladder* or *carpet* yet could remember a fussy little ritual that John seemed to be insisting on more and more these days - but that's another story! He was up the ladder like a monkey, with no regard for safety, grabbing handfuls of yellow loft insulation. "Don't touch the yellow cotton wool stuff," I shouted up to him, "It's dangerous."

"Look, Mum, it's like candy floss!" he shouted down to me. "Must say hello to Golliwog," Sam proceeded to plunder boxes like a demented old tramp until he unearthed the black, gangly one-eyed doll that my mother had naïvely made, completely unaware of all the delicate issues surrounding such a creation. The blue-eyed, blond, wiry twelve-year-old hugging the staring-eyed gangly golliwog looked ludicrous in the half-light of the draughty loft.

"Now for the waistcoat, let me think," said Sam, rubbing his chin pretending to be deep in thought, a mannerism of John's which he had seen many times before. "It must be in here somewhere."

The waistcoat in question was a special one which had been bought from a well known high street store on a hot summer's day in 1995, a very special day for Sam. I remember it well as he had danced down the city centre's main street singing, "It's my lucky day today!" He had proceeded to tell the lady in the Post Office, passers-by on the High Street and shop assistants that he'd been " 'dopted 'day!"

Despite the fact that Sam hadn't made the progress that had been originally expected within the 'eighteen month settling down period', it had become evident that he regarded us as his mum and dad, and as far as Sam was concerned that was that. We had been chosen! Although we still had concerns about his delayed development, neither of us could contemplate moving him to a Children's Home or on to a fifth set of parents and the inevitable trauma and feelings of rejection that would ensue. The fact that we had grown increasingly fond of him, coupled with our desire to protect him, made us realise that we too were beginning to feel like 'real parents' and so the decision was made to proceed with the adoption.

It was on this particular adoption day that everyone in the courtroom had learnt my age, and, had it been left to Sam, the more intimate details of my life. The formality of the courtroom, the red leather chairs embossed with E.R., the clerk of the court's clicking heels echoing down the corridor as she came to fetch us with her black gown billowing behind her, the room full of smartly dressed social workers, the booming command of, "Will the court now rise" as the judge entered, did little to calm the nerves of a hyperactive five year old who proceeded to bury his head in my neck, only staring out with one solemn blue eye.

The judge lightened the atmosphere in the courtroom by saying publicly how much he enjoyed these types of occasions, as it made such a change from his normal routine of sentencing and fining people. I found myself nodding in agreement, as these were similar to the punishments I frequently handed out to Sam!

It seemed obvious to all that before the legalities could proceed the judge wanted to ascertain how Sam felt about the adoption: was he happy, did he like his school, had he got any friends, did he have any pets? Although I knew that Sam was listening to every word he said, I also knew that he didn't fully understand what was going on and was subscribing to the 'if in doubt say nowt!' philosophy. In desperation and frustration the judge turned to me and said,

"When is his birthday?"

"It was my mummy's birthday last week," Sam blurted out, unable to contain himself any more and trying to deflect the attention from himself. The judge, looking both surprised and pleased at this new breakthrough, bent down to look at him over the top of his half moon glasses. "Really, I bet she's not as old as I am," he said trying to draw Sam out.

"No, she's not!" he exclaimed quite categorically. "She's only thirty-nine!" At this the rest of the court smiled sympathetically at this public and brutal exposure of my age, and Sam's apparent ageist attitude towards the judge.

After the tense atmosphere in the courtroom we proceeded to a department store for coffee, cakes and lemonade with our respective social workers. Sam, having been cooped up for so long, and probably galvanised by a great deal of nervous tension, raced around the tables like a demented bluebottle, knocking his lemonade all over John's groin as he raced past. Needless to say, it was a very embarrassed man, who, covering his wet patch with his newspaper, urgently enquired, of the first assistant he encountered, where the men's trousers could be found. "It's not what you think!" he added by way of explanation. "It's only lemonade."

After the new trousers had been quickly substituted for the wet ones, Sam decided that he wanted something new as well. He headed straight for a little navy waistcoat with matching bow-tie to fit a five-year-old and had proceeded to refer to it as his ''doption waistcoat' ever since. Before the 'too small waistcoat' had been relegated to the loft, Sam would appear wearing it with his matching bow tie offering peanuts and crisps to surprised visitors demanding, "Do you want one then?"

It was this waistcoat that Sam was looking for now. You see he had to be 'posh' because he was to play the dad in the class assembly and he wanted to look the part. He had assured his teacher that he had just the very item to look 'posh' in and that was why I was now standing in a draughty loft watching my adopted twelve-year-old son struggle into a navy blue shrunken waistcoat and bow-tie that half strangled him, wondering if I could invent an appointment for 10.25 a.m. on Monday morning!

The waistcoat was half way up his chest as he wandered across the front of the school hall to open an imaginary door to let 'the bear' in. "Oh hello," Sam said to the bear (a boy with fluffy ears and an embarrassed grin) in a nonchalant, this is really beneath me, kind of voice. "Come in."

"There were plenty of other bigger waistcoats he could have chosen from the dressing-up box," his teacher explained apologetically after the 7T assembly, "But he said he wanted to wear that one."

"Yes, it's his special ...." I started, but the teacher's attention had been diverted by another parent intent on telling her how wonderful the assembly had been.

It had been a folk tale which had been dramatized, as is now prescribed in the Literacy hour, but somehow big, awkward adolescent boys dressed up in a pair of net curtains swooping down the central isle of the hall pretending to be the wind didn't quite seem appropriate. A baseball cap on back to front would have helped tremendously!

"Would you like me to take your assembly clothes home?" I tentatively asked Sam.

"No, it's alright, you go," he said dismissively. We were obviously an embarrassment to him in front of his friends despite the fact he hadn't taken his eyes off the two of us for the whole assembly. Just then 'the bear,' minus big fluffy ears, came up to Sam and jumped up, half on, half off his back and gave him a hug. "He's a cheeky monkey he is!" Sam informed us both, with great authority and wisdom beyond his years. The bear just grinned and gave him another enormous hug, as bears are prone to do.

Chapter 11

The Argos voucher was like a shuttlecock, back and forth across the landing, mysteriously transferring itself from my underwear drawer to Sam's bedside table. The Aqua Blast game had been changed twice because the Aqua wouldn't blast and the rubber washer had shrivelled to the size of mouse droppings. The voucher was the replacement for the game and it was this voucher that had kept Sam busy after lights out all week.

Sam still hated reading, books were considered boring but had ceased to be used as missiles to throw across his bedroom. However, there was one special book which proved the exception - the Argos Catalogue. Each page was pored over meticulously. Items of particular interest were sometimes copied down in large, irregular, spidery handwriting, letters and numbers cascading down the page to an indecipherable heap in the bottom right hand corner. Nevertheless, at last he was interested in something, and for the first time was reading and learning about money, the result usually being an early birthday request in April or May for the following October. But fortune had suddenly shone down on him in the form of a meticulous mother who kept every receipt and had therefore managed to produce this £20.00 bonus in the middle of the year.

"I might get these radio controlled telephones," he told me cheerfully.

"But they're £79.99!" I said in dismay at his total lack of mathematical knowledge. "That's nearly £80.00. You've only got £20.00, so that's how much short?"

He's got to be able to do this, I had thought desperately. It's multiples of ten, no units or pennies involved, he'll manage the answer to this. This will boost his self esteem! After five minutes of eyes screwed up as if in deep thought, face turned upwards to the sky as if expecting inspiration to crash down on him from the heavens, we got answers like,"Sixteen pence!" pronounced with great aplomb.

"Sam, it's *pounds* not *pennies*. Remember a hundred pennies make a pound." I tried to keep the urgency out of my voice, as I was forced to face up to the stark reality of how little he could actually remember, despite all those frequent evenings playing shopping games involving changing money and buying things.

"Oh, I'm rubbish I am!" he screamed at me as he stormed out of the kitchen, slamming the door so hard that the whole house shook and the plates on the kitchen shelf wobbled perilously. He swung around the newel post at the bottom of the stairs dangerously fast, just missing my Peace Lily plant by centimetres - it never does much that plant, can't think why! - and proceeded to slam his feet into each riser on the stair, thumping loudly to impress upon us how cross he really was. Then into the familiar angry routine of duvet thrown off the bed across the door to stop anyone entering - as if anyone would want to! - closely followed by pillows and finally bottom sheet (perhaps he was going in for the champion bed-stripping finals?) I could now picture the scene, Sam stretched out across the bed, arms folded across his chest, a grey frown troubling his forehead and bottom lip thrust out in grumpy gesture of defiance.

"It's his cerebellum that's delayed in its development," the DDAT (Dyslexia, Dyspraxia, Attention Deficit) Centre in Kenilworth had informed us after a long trek up the motorway on a cold and grey day at Easter time. "The astronauts suffered mildly from dyslexia when they came back from space and NASA devised a series of balancing exercises to help eradicate it. Try these exercises with your son. It could help to improve his condition. We've had a lot of success." Certainly the letters around the waiting room walls were testament to that, but everyone else's child seemed to want to improve in the first place, not to turn this into a control issue as Sam frequently did.

"Sam, it says sit up straight on the stool, not slump forwards like an obese gorilla with flatulence. Now come on, you've really got to stretch your arms to the left without losing your balance on the stool," I said encouragingly to Sam as we laboriously waded through his daily exercise routine before and after school each day. "Stretch your arm to the right. That's not stretching. Come on, concentrate!"

"Oh, do we have to?" Sam implored, his arm hanging loosely and pathetically as if it didn't belong to him.

"Well if you don't try, I'm having that Argos Voucher on Saturday. We need some things for the garden."

"Have it then, I don't care!" he'd shouted and the kitchen door took another battering as he slammed out and shouted his way to his room.

Later, when he was asleep, I'd taken the voucher from his bedside table and hidden it in my underwear drawer. He'll never think of looking there, I thought gleefully. The next morning, in an attempt to put all the previous night's hassles behind us, we'd tried to wrestle Sam out of his usual early morning 'mood' by reminding him of the previous night's viewing on TV.

"Come on, James Bond," John, had yelled in an attempt to rouse him. "You're on a challenging mission this morning. You have five minutes to wash, clean teeth, comb hair and eat your breakfast. Go!" As usual, nothing happened. The lump under the duvet lay motionless. "Come on! If you're going to take over from

Pierce Brosnan and save the world, you're going to have to be more dynamic than that!"

"Get lost!" came the muffled reply.

"Come on ...!" John continued undaunted, "Miss Moneypenny will be here soon to collect you!"

Miss Moneypenny was Sam's morning taxi driver, she was round and dumpy, had a tongue which could cut steel and more importantly, let him play Snake on her mobile for the whole journey to school.

He was up in a flash, moving around the house like greased lightning, slamming the front door as he heard the car horn, the Peace Lily quivering in the down-draught as he tore out. 'Phew, now for some peace and quiet' I thought, as I plodded upstairs to make the beds. That's when I found the voucher, back on his bedside table.

Chapter 12

I locked the front door in the nick of time as the taxi swept into the drive and within seconds the front door handle was being rattled and shaken within an inch of its life. "What did you lock the door for, Mum?" asked Sam as he came in the side door.

Always anticipating rejection, I answered him quickly and cheerfully. "Ah well, I'd remembered that you'd been on a coastal walk and I was trying to save my carpets from being covered in mud." It was Activity Week at school and he'd been tramping down one of the coastal paths with his class. "Had a good day then?" I asked quickly to avoid him dwelling on any ulterior motive for locking the door (which there wasn't) and my heart sank when I was greeted with silence. Silence was bad, it meant trouble with a capital T. Our normal exchange went something like this.

"Had a good day. Sam?"

"Yeh, fine."

"Any homework?"

"No, none can I have a biscuit is Dad home yet?" This was usually said all in one breath in order to deflect me from the sticky subject of homework, but tonight it was different!

"Come on! What's happened?" I asked, thoughts of suspensions and exclusions flashing through my mind. "Tell me! Come on!" I encouraged. I hated nights like these as I had to psychologically rearrange myself in order to remain calm, whatever might be forthcoming.

It all had started on a school trip as the children had been walking in a crocodile up the pavement. The girl behind had decided to hit Sam with her empty water bottle. According to Sam he had done exactly as we had told him, and ignored her. My heart swelled with pride.

After the years of over-reaction we had experienced, he was finally getting the message! And to prove our point the teacher had actually turned round and admonished her. The girl had then continued to hit him across the head with her bottle and so Sam had taken it upon himself to give her what was commonly known at school as a 'dead arm'. At that point, a big bruiser of a lad in year 10, had decided it was his job to defend his sister and had asked Sam if he had hit her. Faced with this, Sam's courage had deserted him and he had said that he hadn't. Bad move!

"Why didn't you tell the truth?" I asked him, " You were in the right. The teacher had told her off. You had nothing to worry about" I said encouragingly.

"Because he'd have hit me and he's bigger than me!" Sam had exclaimed with a contempt which implied I knew nothing about anything.

"Well, he did that anyway," I said, five minutes later, as I was frantically trying to sequence the events. I'd got lost at the part where the deputy headmaster had had to tear them apart.

Sam had stomped off in a temper because he knew that the deputy head wouldn't listen to him. "Because they always take the other side, they never listen to me!" he said in disgust.

I knew what he meant because I had done it myself when he'd had friends round to play. Because other children were so very quick to find the weak spot, they would often take delight in deliberately trying to wind Sam up. After years of training, Sam had finally stopped over- reacting and now just came to adults with a constant stream of tales instead! Those poor teachers, I thought to myself, no wonder there's a shortage! Nevertheless, I knew I had to do something about it or it could easily spill over into the next day. I felt it important that someone at school should talk out what had happened with Sam, to quell any sense of outrage that could develop if he felt he hadn't been properly 'heard'.

I always hated ringing up school in case they thought I was one of those neurotic mothers with completely unrealistic expectations about what could really be achieved with a class of children with mild learning difficulties. I frequently seemed to play down the actual problem in order to hide my real anxieties, I always had to brace myself in case I had to defend him, against any other accusations which might be forthcoming, and about which Sam hadn't told me.

"I'm sorry, the headmaster has just left, along with the Deputy, to go to a meeting and the head of Key Stage 3 is on a residential all week," the breathless, friendly lady at the other end of the phone informed me.

"Such a pity," I replied, with frustration, "Could you take a message for me, do you think?"

"Just a minute, while I get a pen." I hung on.

I ought to have guessed that there might be a problem with the retelling of the tale in the morning by the number of times she stopped and asked me to spell words, and the snail's pace at which she was recording the tale.

"Well thank you for offering to pass all that on for me," I said, trying to bring the conversation to a close. "I'm sorry to burden you with all this so late on in the school day," I smarmed gratefully. "Could you just give me your name, so that I know who I've been speaking to?" I asked carefully, in anticipation of retracing my steps the next day.

"Oh, I'm just Enid !" she'd replied, laughing, "But I'll tell 'im, luvver, don't you worry!" she reassured me in her rich West Country accent. The tension drained from me as I realised that for the last ten minutes I'd been carefully and thoughtfully defending my son's actions to none other than the school cleaner!

He was finishing watching his favourite television programme when I decided to try to retrieve something positive from the day's events.

"Actually I think you did really well not to over-react today," I began. "Because you ignored that girl in the first place. you didn't get into trouble and she did!" I told him triumphantly. "But maybe you shouldn't have hit her brother first when he was calling you names?" I suggested tentatively, "And maybe you shouldn't have stomped off when the deputy headmaster came to pull you apart," I added surprised that I'd managed to get all that out without Sam interrupting me indignantly with his side of the story. "So, what would you do differently next time?" I asked pushing my luck.

"I shouldn't have stropped off when the deputy headmaster came," he replied with a big bored sigh which implied, she's off again. "But," he continued justifying his actions, "her brother didn't care whether he was there or not, he just kept on hitting me and I wasn't going to take that, I was getting out of there fast!" I marvelled at his powers of self preservation, as I had done many times over the nine years that we had had him.

I consulted the calendar. Eight weeks since the last lot of *Tuberculinum* which was supplied by the local homeopath. Obviously time for another tablet, I mused. These little white tablets had kept us sane over the past five years. It was hard to believe that one of these dissolved under the tongue could make such a difference to Sam's behaviour: it would act within a day, changing him from a hyperactive twelve year old to a calmer and more rational boy. I rang the number and placed my order over the phone. We were on first name terms by now and greeted each other like old friends,

"And how are you?" the homeopath asked, "Still sleeping alright?"

I hesitated before answering, as my sleep pattern was like one of those computer screens at the side of a patient's bed in a hospital drama, sometimes up, sometimes in the middle, but often bumping along the bottom!

"I wouldn't mind something to calm me down," I'd replied. Perhaps I was developing the symptoms of ADHD too, I thought, as I plodded off to get the tea ready! As I opened the cupboard door I spotted the brown bag that had been sitting there for the last five years, the bag that I kept in case the *Tuberculinum* stopped working, in case I got desperate. The bag I'd vowed I'd never use. The dreaded Ritalin bag! It lurked ominously. Not yet, I told myself, and pushed it to the back of the cupboard and firmly closed the door.

Chapter 13

"It's Linda's birthday today," Sam announced as he chomped through his Cornflakes, greasy hair stuck in fingers across his head, a grey look to his teenage skin.

"Sam, have you had a shower this morning?" I asked. I think I'll just make a tape recording and press play at 8.10 am every morning, I thought to myself as I stared at the unwashed teenager in despair.

"Yeh, I have!" he said antagonistically.

"You haven't had a proper shower," I heard myself repeating like a robot, "You may have stood under the water, but you haven't washed yourself at all, and you certainly haven't washed your hair!" Sometimes I looked forward to the day that he would start to take an interest in girls. At least we might catapult him out of the ranks of the great unwashed, I thought longingly.

"Why didn't you do the card for Linda's birthday last night?" I asked him, trying to move the conversation along before we got stuck in a negative confrontation about washing.

"I thought I'd do it this morning," he replied without looking up from his cornflake bowl, which was awash with milk.

"But have you seen the time?"

"I know, I know, I'll do it in a minute."

I don't think he'll ever be able to think ahead and organize himself, I thought glumly as I watched Linda, Sam's taxi driver, sweep up the drive to take him off to school.

"Good news!" He burst through the front door, all thoughts of birthday cards forgotten. "Guess what?" Without giving us time to guess, he tore onwards, "I'm in the school football team!" he announced, triumphant, "and we've got a match next Wednesday afternoon."

You'd have thought that he had been picked for the world cup squad, he was so excited. "Who are you playing?" I asked. Sam answered with the name of a completely undecipherable school, which we eventually unravelled as being the nearest Special School in the neighbouring area.

"And we're going to thrash 'em. Six Nil. Six Nil." he began chanting, as he ran down the hallway, jumping up to head the ceiling light into an imaginary goal. "And he's scored, Yessssss!" he shouted as he disappeared into the sitting room.

The next week consisted of finding lost football valves, retrieving balls from neighbours' gardens and constant practice across the drive. John was out there every night trying to teach him the basic rules of football, mainly the importance of remembering which way his team was shooting, remembering to pass and not hog the ball, and a peppering of football skills. They did heading, shooting, and dribbling, and after a week John declared that he wasn't that bad. Although his fine motor skills were delayed, making progress in reading and writing painfully slow, we had been told that the other side of his brain over-compensated which meant that ice skating, skiing, horse riding and any sport which required balance seemed to come naturally. However, despite his good sense of balance, we were still worried about the match. We knew that Sam's inability to remember things and his poor concentration meant that he risked letting the side down.

The day dawned and we both awoke with butterflies in our stomachs. John had rearranged his schedule and managed to take time off to watch the match. We stood on the draughty school field with our coats wrapped around us as the school minibus came into view. There was Sam waving madly, a big cheesy grin spreading from ear to ear. Already John could hear him shouting, "That's my dad," through the bus window.

When the bus finally came to a standstill, Sam exploded out with half the school team behind him. Our faces erupted in a grin when we saw what Sam was wearing. The three lions of England that were meant to rest on his front left thigh were happily jogging along across his backside!

"Sam!" we whispered urgently, " You've got your shorts on back to front. Quick, go into the minibus and swap them over!"

"Get lost!" he'd replied, full of bravado in front of his team mates, "There's girls on that bus, I'm not getting changed in there!" He was right, there were girls in the bus, and as all football teams have to be PC nowadays and include both sexes, Sam was in a fix.

"And look at your football shirt," John had continued in alarm , "It's at least two sizes too small and it's all twisted round. You look like you've screwed your head on the wrong way this afternoon," he whispered, trying to jolt Sam into doing something about the way he looked. The only things that were on correctly were the new boots bought on Saturday, then proudly taken to school to show all the interested, or otherwise, teachers who then had to guess how much they had cost.

Most of them, being used to the normal over-indulged middle class child, had given the answers they thought Sam wanted.

"Seventy pounds," the science teacher had answered without great interest.

"A hundred pounds," the headmaster had obligingly replied.

"No!" said Sam, full of triumph that they hadn't managed to guess, "Seven pounds! That's all they cost! We got them in the sale." Fortunately for us, Sam had not yet realised the importance of having the right trainers at the right price, if you were to have any street cred at all.

Sam's team ran onto the field like a bunch of excited puppies. The teacher gave a quick blast on his whistle and tried to gather them all together for a quick pre-match talk. Sam was so excited that he was practicing his latest judo punches and not listening to a word the teacher said.

"Ryan, you're in goal, so remember to narrow your angles." John panicked. If Ryan could narrow his angles, then he was going to be a much better player than Sam, who couldn't even get his shorts on the right way round!

"Jason, remember to switch wings when you're attacking." Sam was still punching an imaginary judo opponent on the edge of the group.

"Sam, stand still!" his teacher ordered, "Now, you remember you're in defence, so you need to stay well back" he commanded authoritatively. It all seemed a bit much for a group of children with learning difficulties but nevertheless they all lined up for the kick off. Hearts were pounding and adrenalin was rushing but Sam was still finishing off his imaginary judo opponent!

"Sam!" John shouted through his hands, "Why are you standing on the goal line? Move up!" he bellowed trying to keep the panic out of his voice.

"Mr. Wates told me to stay well back, don't you know anything about football?" he shouted at John with disgust in his voice. The game started. We felt anxious. Would his lack of understanding make him look silly? I couldn't watch.

It was remarkable. For seven minutes Sam did

as he was told and stayed back near the goal line. The play was all in the opponents' half and Sam, bored with judo throws, had graduated to cartwheels on the goal line. The goalie was not impressed and even he kept on hissing at Sam to concentrate. Suddenly, Sam had had enough. As if someone had flicked a switch he decided he had to get involved in the game! He ran thirty yards like a bullet from a gun, frustration having got the better of him, determined to have a go. Despite playing in a defensive position he attacked well and with real purpose and I began to realise that he had a lot more skill than I had given him credit for. I even began to feel a little optimistic. He played a major part in getting possession of the ball at one point and I began to feel quite emotional when he passed the ball across from the right wing to enable his team to score.

"Well played," we roared in unison. Tears glinted in my eyes as I realised our son had actually worked as part of the team and managed to do something constructive. Then, panic! The ball was suddenly swept down the field while Sam was still celebrating with his shirt pulled over his head at the other end! Sam was suddenly jerked from his celebrations by the goalie shouting "Where's my defence?"

Wherever he was he wasn't quick enough and the opposition scored. One all! All communicaton between the goalie and his defence had now broken down. They were just snarling insults at each other until Sam was off again, like a terrier after a rabbit, dribbling the ball past three players, crossing the ball from the other wing this time, allowing a second goal for Sam's team to hit the net. Two - One! Goalie and Sam were speaking again! Sam romped on, taking corner kicks, throw ins, free kicks - none of which were in his job description, but oh! we were so proud of his energy, his stamina, his obvious enjoyment, and his sense of fun. It was then that I realised that I was jealous of him, jealous of his ability to really throw himself into the situation oblivious to everyone and enjoy himself. He was laughing, having such fun and the time of his life. Unaware of the restrictions which had been placed on him, he was just enjoying being with others, running with the ball, tackling, shooting, dribbling - scoring goals was incidental. For the first time in his life he felt that he belonged, he was part of a team and they were working together.

Suddenly he got possession of the ball and ran up the field dribbling his way easily past two opponents towards the edge of the penalty area with only the goalie to beat. Abruptly he stopped, was he remembering why he was out there after all?

"Go on Sam, keep going!" John was shouting. "Follow through and shoot!" But it was too late: he who hesitates is lost. Sam hesitated too long and the ball was gone.

"Why did you stop at the edge of the penalty area?" John asked later that night.

"I don't know, I forgot," said Sam, "I didn't know if I was allowed in there, I couldn't remember. Anyway it didn't matter - we still won, five three. Five three! Five three!" he chanted as he walked down the hall, muddied up to the eyebrows, with his shorts still on back-to-front!

Chapter 14

In an effort to boost Sam's self-esteem, John put his name down for a paper round, something which they could initially do together and which would, more importantly, give him that bit of extra independence and pocket money. Another motive was that it guaranteed at least one hour's fresh air and exercise every day, something that was in increasingly short supply now that Sam had acquired a playstation for his thirteenth birthday. The introductory period lasted a week, during which the incumbent, who was giving up to spend more time with his GCSE coursework, would show Sam the ropes.

Being anxious that Sam wouldn't remember what he was told John volunteered to go round with them so as to listen in to any instructions, working on the proviso that two heads are better than one.

"No way!" was Sam's disgusted response, appalled at being shown up by an ageing father tagging on behind. "I'll be fine!"

"Well, listen carefully to what he tells you." had been John's unconvinced response. "And mind the roads!"

The first week past in a flash, the novelty of going out with a much older boy proved fun for Sam and he came back breathless, animated and alert at the end of each session. "Has it gone OK?" we quizzed him on his return each evening.

"Yeh, fine," he responded as if he didn't know what all the fuss was about. On the last day John, running the risk of being completely cold shouldered by Sam, went along to see what would be expected of him the following week when he would be on his own.

"He's having trouble folding the papers properly," the retiring paper boy had told John. "I keep showing him but he still keeps getting it wrong," he said, trying to keep the amusement out of his voice. He had obviously become quite fond of Sam, but realised that he didn't pick things up easily. "He's got to fold them vertically so that they slip through the letter boxes more easily. He keeps folding them horizontally and it makes them a difficult shape to get through the box," he finished, with a grin at Sam.

"I know," said Sam, looking embarrassed, "I just keep forgetting, that's all!" He was obviously cross with himself and embarrassed at the exposure of his weaknesses in front of a virtual stranger whom he admired and thought 'cool.'

"We'll practice, we'll soon sort that out," John quickly reassured the retiring paperboy. "Is there anything else before you sign off?"

"Well, there's the old peoples' home."

"Pardon?" enquired John hoping that he had misheard. He knew Sam had taken his toll but he didn't think he looked that bad!

"The old peoples' home," the boy reiterated, " You need to remember a pin number to get inside the main doors. There's three old people that have a paper in there."

"A pin number?" repeated John in horror. "How many digits does it have?"

"Six," he added and then proceeded to reel them off all in one breath. " I've told Sam to write them down somewhere so he can remember them, but he keeps getting them in the wrong order!"

"I'll write them in the telephone book," announced Sam in an unconcerned voice.

"The phone book!" said John in panic, "Why the phone book?"

"Well, that's where you write numbers you want to

remember," he replied, incredulous at John's stupidity.

"Yes, but you're not lugging our phone book round with you on your paper round every day," said John, aghast at Sam's lack of problem-solving skills. "We'll have to think of another way of remembering it. If you lose that or post it through someone's letter box by mistake, the whole family's scuppered!"

"Here's my oldest paperboy!" the friendly newsagent declared the following day to a shop full of amused people as John strode in to collect the papers.

Sam struggled with his padlock outside on the pavement. He'd had a new bike for his birthday, as his old one was an embarrassment alongside all the other paperboys' full- suspension, shiny well-cared-for, top-of-the-range bikes.

"I'll go round with him for the first week," John had volunteered, "I want to check that he knows what he's doing. I don't want the newsagent ringing up with loads of complaints about papers in the wrong box!" John told me, in confidence, on Sam's first day.

"I'm only coming for the exercise," John had reassured Sam. "I need to lose some weight, so it will do me good and I'll ride fifty yards behind you if that makes you less embarrassed," he added.

"The papers are all marked up in the sequence that they should be delivered. There's either numbers or house names scrawled on the top and I've put the pin number on the old peoples' papers. I'll do it for the first week and then he'll have to remember," the newsagent added. "Have fun!" she shouted after John, as he strode out of the shop, with the fluorescent yellow sack, bulging with papers, across his back.

"You've given me the wrong paper!" shouted the tall erect man who was striding down the pebbled sweeping drive with a unwanted newspaper in his hand.

"Mine's the *Times*!" he said curtly implying that any fool could get it right, so why couldn't Sam?

"Sorry," muttered Sam humbly. At this point John popped out from behind the hedge where he had been hiding in his attempt to withdraw his support gradually, as the first week of Sam's round was now drawing to a close.

"You've got them mixed up. Remember Ashford Lodge has the *Mail* and Ashford House has the *Times*," he explained patiently to Sam.

"O.K." said the man more calmly, obviously reassured by John's presence, "Thank you." And with that he crunched back up his sweeping gravelled drive.

"You've got to try to read the names of the houses on the top of the paper," John had gently tried to remind Sam without undermining his confidence. "The newsagent does give them to you in the correct order. I know that you are trying to do the round purely by memory, but it might just help if you glance down now and again and check that the right paper is going through the right door," he suggested as diplomatically as he could.

"I know, I know," replied Sam, his confidence obviously shaken.

I sat listening to the clock's steady ticks as I pretended to read. In reality, I was really expecting the phone to ring at any moment. Then I heard it - not the phone, but the insistent wail of the siren which seemed to be getting nearer and nearer. Panic,! Was it an ambulance? Only the day before I had taken Sam out on his bike and made him cycle the newspaper route in preparation for his first day solo, only to be appalled by the speed at which he seemed to approach busy road junctions, using his brakes to squeal to a halt with only centimetres to spare before the hurly-burly of the main road. Maybe he had had an accident? I went to the phone. It was no good. I would just have to reassure myself and risk his wrath and accusations of fussing. I rang his mobile number and counted the rings as each one rang out.

"It wasn't me, Mum!" came the panicked response, "I just pressed the keys on the door panel, and the alarms went off as I was walking in!"

"Where are you?" I questioned.

"I'm at the old peoples' home," he replied with exasperation that I didn't automatically know where he was. "I got the right pin number 'cos I keyed it into my mobile so that I could remember it. As I was walking down the corridor the fire alarms went off. I didn't do it. Honest!" he added in obvious panic.

"Of course you didn't do it," I tried to reassure him, "How could you have set the fire alarms off? It must have been pure coincidence - that's all. If you pressed the right buttons on the entrance panel it wouldn't set the fire alarms off," I tried to reassure him again.

"I know that's what I said."

"To whom?" I replied in panic. It was sounding more serious by the minute.

"Some kids that are standing watching the fire engine said that I'd done it when I was inside delivering the papers." He tried to sound unconcerned, but I could tell that he was worried.

Although I knew Sam well enough to know that the trauma of his first day on his own delivering the papers would be enough for him to cope with, without the added complication of setting off fire alarms, I thought I'd better check just in case.

"Well? Did you?"

"Mum!" He was disgusted that I even thought that

he might have done it and he was disappointed with my apparent low opinion of him.

"Sorry, just checking. Do you want me to come up and finish your round with you?"

"No, I'll be fine," he added, as if that would be the ultimate embarrassment for him.

"Well, take it steady and watch the roads," I reminded him, relieved that he was alright.

"They've brought my old lady out, Mum," said Sam, still keeping up the running commentary on the phone. "The firemen are bringing all the old people out and standing them on the pavement, Mum."

"What do you mean - your old lady?" I asked, having had enough drama for one afternoon.

"There's an old lady that waits for me every day and talks to me. She calls me 'Smiler' and asks me what I've been up to and things." Obviously not thinking it important enough to mention before, he added "The sprinklers have come on in the rooms and everything is getting wet, so they've had to come outside for a bit. Shall I bring her home for a cup of tea?"

I felt proud of his spontaneous compassion and gentle caring nature which was becoming an ever more prominent feature of his evolving personality.

"I'm sure she'll enjoy being with all those handsome firemen much more than she would being with me," I said, ducking the issue, and feeling, not for the first time, that Sam could teach me a thing or two about public spiritedness and compassion.

"Dad, help! I've got them muddled up and I've pushed them in the wrong box!"

"Hang on, don't panic, we'll sort it out," John spoke calmly and tried to reassure him.

"Where are you?" John nodded, then, as he put

down the phone, turned to me and said,

"He's nearly in tears, he's got them muddled up again. I'm going to have to go knocking on doors and ask people for their papers back. This is going to be so embarrassing!" I was just glad that it was a Saturday and that John was around to field the call.

"He was in a real state when I got there," John told me later that evening. "I just had to knock on peoples' doors and ask for the papers back. Most were fine when I explained that it was only his first week out by himself and he'd got confused, some even saw the funny side. The only one that didn't was the man at Ashford House. It was a good job that I got there in time, otherwise he would have knocked his confidence completely," said John, lost in thought, reliving the incident in his mind.

"He came marching down the drive at full pelt and you could see that he was really angry. Sam was going up the drive to try and retrieve the paper from the letter box and didn't see him at first.

" 'You've done it again!' he shouted. 'You've given me the wrong paper. Despite me telling you, you're still getting it wrong!' " Sam was shrinking back against the hedge. He was frightened, so I thought I'd better intervene quickly.

" 'I'm dreadfully sorry,' I said. 'But my son is badly dyslexic and it takes him longer to learn things than other children.' " The man's stance changed instantly, 'I'm extremely sorry,' he said, seeming genuinely full of remorse, 'I do apologise. I didn't realise.' "

" 'Apology accepted,' I said. 'Mind you, I must admit I'd get upset, if someone delivered the *Mail* instead of the *Times* to my house!' And we both parted laughing, so situation defused, I think," said John, still chuckling at his own joke.

It was three months later when all folding practice had been completed, pin numbers memorised and Lodges and Houses had been sorted out, that the next problem had to be dealt with. As Sam had now proved a steady employee, he had been asked to cover an evening round for a couple of weeks.

It was one of those early spring evenings, when you suddenly begin to notice how light it still is at 5 o'clock; instead of drawing the curtains to shut out the night you begin to think about all those jobs that have accumulated over the winter months. People were out washing their cars, reluctant to waste a minute of the early spring sunshine, on their return from work. I was aware of the voices of children playing out in the streets, then I heard the dull thud of the kitchen door, as Sam returned from his paper round.

As soon as he came into the sitting room I could tell by the look on his face that something was very wrong,

"I'm giving it up! I'm not doing it anymore!" he shouted in anger as he tried to hold back the tears, his face a dark beetroot red. I noticed that the back of his fleece was covered in grass. On closer inspection of his face, I found two bruises and a cut.

"What has been happening?" I asked, trying to keep the shock and concern out of my voice.

"It's Jason, and that friend of his Carl, they wouldn't let me finish my round, *and* they pulled me off my bike and thumped me! That's it, I'm finishing my round forever!" With that he broke into tears of humiliation and distress.

"Sam, this is serious," I said, shocked at what he had just told me, angry that all the months of hard work building up his self esteem had apparently been smashed in one fell swoop by a group of little thugs who lived in a poorer housing area at the end of his round. "Tell me carefully what happened, because I think this might be a matter for the police. It isn't normal, what has happened to you, and I think we should report it."

Through gulps of embarrassed and angry recollection, Sam recounted the last, seemingly endless, ten minutes of his round, while I attempted to assess the extent of his injuries and to calm him down.

"I was coming to the end of my round. I only had one more paper to deliver. I was cycling round the corner when there were six boys blocking my way. They said that I couldn't pass their line and said that they would finish off delivering the papers. I said no way and that I'd got to do them 'cos I thought they might throw them away or something."

"You're right, Sam, they probably would have," I concurred.

"But they wouldn't let me pass. Then they said that they would let me deliver the papers while they looked after my bike and I said 'No way' 'cos they'd have nicked my bike!"

"You're right again, Sam, they probably would. Didn't you think to just ride through them and try to get away as quickly as possible?" I asked.

"Mum, I couldn't!" he exclaimed bursting into tears again, as he recalled the hopelessness of the situation. "Then one of them said to get off their patch and did I want a fight and I said no and would they please let me deliver my papers?" He blurted it out all in one breath.

"And what happened then?" I asked.

"That's when the fat one pulled me off my bike and hit me. I tried to stick up for myself but there were too many of them. So, as soon as I could, I got back on my bike and pedalled like mad to get away."

Ten minutes later, once I was certain that Sam

had told me everything, I rang up to report the incident. "This sounds like quite a serious assault," the policeman at the other end of the phone said. "We'll be sending someone round to talk to your son about what happened later on this evening."

"Couldn't someone come round now?" I asked, angry at the delay. "I'm sure a quick swish round the area with a police car wouldn't come amiss."

"Sorry, madam," came the polite response, "We operate on a strict order-of-priority basis and someone will be round to interview your son some time this evening. We are really busy at the moment."

Nobody felt like eating any tea that evening and we all felt that our lives were on hold until we had had an opportunity to discuss the incident with the police. Two and a half hours later the phone rang. The person at the other end asked to speak to me. After taking down the particulars of where, when, who and why, the latter being the most difficult to answer, we came to the conclusion that having remembered Sam from primary School days, they had decided to have some fun with him, realising that he wasn't that bright. After clarifying clearly what had happened with Sam, the police lady asked to be transferred back to me.

"Does your son need hospital treatment?" she enquired.

"No, he needed treatment, but I have dealt with it. I don't think he needs to go to hospital," I reassured her.

"The problem is," she continued, "That, as you say Sam has difficulties with his writing, it is going to be hard to get a written statement from him. It will mean coming down to the station and videoing the verbal report. That won't be a very nice experience for him. He will also have to have a social worker present."

The last thing we wanted to do was drag Sam down to the local police station at ten o' clock at night to do a video interview on top of the traumatic day he had already had.

"What's the alternative?" I asked, angry at the delay in getting back to us, a delay which seemed to add insult to injury by trivializing the incident.

"You could certainly press charges if you wanted to. We've got all the names, but what I would suggest we do is monitor the situation really closely. If there are further incidents, even the slightest thing, such as name calling, anything at all provocative, then I would go ahead and press charges. It also wouldn't hurt to let those concerned know that we have names," she added knowingly.

"What! I hope you have reported it to the police!" exclaimed the shocked newsagent as we recounted the incident the next day, when John went to collect the papers and to explain Sam's reticence about delivering the papers that day. "Never in all my days has one of my paperboys been attacked like that! I'm not having that!" she said in disgust. "Who did it? I want names. I've been a newsagent for thirty years in this shop and never have we had an incident like this before. Give me their names." she demanded again. "I'll sort'em out and I'll see their mothers!" she stated with determination. "You're not going to give up on me, are you?" she asked, turning to look at Sam, and giving him an encouraging smile. "I don't know," she sighed, "What is the world coming to?"

"Well, you can tell them when you see them, that the police have been notified, and that they have names, and if there is any repetition of that behaviour, we will have no hesitation in pressing charges," John said. "And it might be useful if you could alter the last part of his round because he is scared to go into that area again on his own. He has lost a lot of confidence through all of this."

"Leave it with me, I'll put one of the more experienced lads on it," she said, reassuringly.

Four weeks later Sam burst into the kitchen after completing his round, one Saturday evening, eyes sparkling, rosy-cheeked and triumphant.

"Look what I've got!" he declared placing a large chocolate Easter egg on the kitchen table.

"Where's that from?" I asked, intrigued, but delighted that his confidence had apparently returned and that he was happy to do his round again.

"My old lady gave it me," he said proudly. "She said I was her favourite paper boy 'cos I'm cheerful. She said that it's for Easter Day tomorrow," he declared. "Can I have a bit now mum?" he asked.

"Well, just a bit, it's nearly tea time," I answered trying to hide a smile.

"I think she's a bit confused," whispered John, when Sam was well out of earshot. " Easter isn't for another five weeks. "Still, I can see why they get on, they're both as confused about time as each other!"

Chapter 15

"Eat your Bran Flakes, Sam!" I shouted crossly as he stirred them around the bowl with obvious disinterest.

"I don't like them!" he answered petulantly, "They're a pain in the backside!"

"Well, that's what you'll get if you don't eat them!" I admonished, pleased with my little joke, but at the same time recalling our recent visit to the doctor who had recommended that Sam should start the day with them. Our attempt to try to get him to take responsibility for his own health and well being had fallen on deaf ears, and so it was our job to make sure his diet contained enough roughage and also to make sure that he was drinking enough. These additional responsibilities we welcomed like a hole in the head, but it had been while we had been on holiday for a two week break, and had spent extended periods of time together, that we realised how little fluid Sam actually drank. It was then suggested that his periods of hyperactivity could be due to a build-up of toxins in his body, hence the constant reminders to drink. We were not concerned, however, about the amount of exercise Sam was getting!

I had noticed how lethargic and tired Sam had been recently on returning home from school - most unlike him, as he always seemed to have plenty of energy.

"Is there anything you've been doing at school to make you tired?" I asked him, concerned.

"Running, I've been running," he said, "All dinner time I have been running."

"Why?" I asked, "What have you been running from?"

"A girl at school, she likes me, and she keeps chasing me!" he said with absolute loathing. He wasn't into girls at all, despite being quite a handsome boy. "Ugh!"

"You can't spend the whole dinner time running away from her," I said, "It's one and a quarter hours long. You can't spend all that time running away." I realised that he meant what he said.

"Mum, I have to or she'll try to kiss me! Yuck!" he said with disgust.

"Well, can't you tell a dinner lady?" I asked.

"Mum, it's no good, they just stand there gossiping, they don't take any notice at all. I keep going to tell them but they just tell me to go away!"

"Well, this girl who keeps on chasing you, what's she called?" I asked, envisaging ringing up the school the next day, to ask them to keep an eye on the situation.

"Tracey, she's called Tracey."

"Well what's she like, this Tracey, is she nice?" I asked, trying to interject a positive note into the proceedings.

"She's small and fat, with a red face. She wears little boots with clicky heels, and rolls her skirt up at the top to make it short!" he said with disdain.

"Keep on running, son!" I said, suddenly grasping the situation. "Keep on running!"

It was just after Sam's thirteenth birthday that we began to notice an improvement in his language skills, an apparently subconscious absorption of language, demonstrated by Sam often supplying the appropriate word in the correct context, but without necessarily understanding its meaning.

While talking to John in the front of the car about a current piece of work that I was undertaking and trying to explain the problems I was having with it, Sam suddenly tuned into our conversation.

"I have got about halfway through with it," I was

saying to John, "And I need a quick overview or a mini....
mini..." I stopped as I searched for the correct word.

"ISA." interjected Sam, " You need a mini ISA."

"Blimey, you can tell it's April, can't you?" John
sniggered.

Unfortunately Sam's writing still lagged well
behind his reading, as is usually the case. Having waved
our rather exuberant and drunken neighbours off the
premises one Saturday evening, I staggered upstairs.
There was a written note stuck on Sam's bedroom door.
I was overjoyed. I couldn't believe my eyes. He was
actually communicating because he wanted to. Normally
he had to be persuaded, cajoled and bribed to write a
sentence a day and even that was a real struggle. It read,
'Quiut plesa, I'm asleeping' The spelling left a lot to be
desired, but, nevertheless, my eyes momentarily filled
with tears and my mind with hope, as I inwardly rejoiced
at the apparent small but definite lurches forward sam
was making.

We now noticed a change in Sam's preferred
weekend activities. The usual pattern had been to tear
up and down the road playing imaginary games with the
other children, which often resulted in unusual requests
like, 'Can I borrow the tow rope?' and 'Have you got
any feathers?' When interrupted from this particularly
frantic activity, he had informed me that he was busy
tying a Native American squaw to a totem pole (lamp
post) and would I please pass him his cowboy hat? Now
we noticed how interested he became when John was
engaged in practical activities, like servicing the lawn
mower, cementing the path and - particularly - any
activity which involved sawing, hammering or knocking
in nails.

"He's amazing!" John would come in from the garage
shaking his head, "He seems to know exactly which tool

to pass me, even before I've had the chance to work it out for myself! I actually picked up the wrong tool from the tool box the other day and he said, 'That's the wrong one, Dad, you need this one' and passed me the right tool!"

The down-side to this, of course, was that whenever John went to look for a specific tool, it was often missing, as Sam seemed pathologically predisposed never to return things to their proper place. Thoroughly irritated by the situation, John, having succumbed as usual to a gadget from the monthly catalogue that regularly landed on the mat, took delivery of a new tool on a handle with a screw-in angled blade, designed to cut weeds from between the cracks in paving slabs. Knowing that Sam would be onto it like lightning, he carefully hid it behind some garden canes in a darkened corner of the garage while Sam was at school.

"I just don't believe it!" shouted John, sounding more and more like Victor Meldrew every day.

"Come and look at this!" he said, almost dragging me to the window. There was Sam, back bent, intent on getting all the weeds out from between the bricks in the red block bricked sweeping road, which served the whole *cul-de-sac*.

"Look!" exclaimed John, "Not only has he managed to find it, but he knows exactly what to do with it. I just don't believe it!"

We noticed this ability to pre-empt in other situations, like cooking and sewing, whereby he would instinctively seem to know what to pass me when I most needed it, despite never having done it before. He seemed to have developed a sixth sense, always wanting to be two jumps ahead, trying to anticipate events before they actually happened.

"Maybe it's a kind of anxiety caused by his constant

shifting between carers in his early years. Maybe it developed from the need to look after himself when he was too young?" I ventured, trying to account for his unusual ability. Whatever it was, we just hoped that it would stand him in good stead in later life when his practical skills could be developed to help him earn his living.

Sam continued to provide a lot of fun and amusement in our lives, and those of our extended family, when we managed to meet together, despite the distance between us. On a family weekend to the Isle of Wight, when aunties, uncles, cousins and grannies were present, we had, after much deliberation - trying to accommodate a day out for three generations wasn't easy - decided to spend the day looking around the house and gardens of Osborne House, the home of the late Queen Victoria. As we wound our way around the grand and richly decorated halls, rooms and corridors, we couldn't help noticing and commenting on the beautiful bronze statues that frequently decorated the alcoves and tables. We were overheard by a quietly spoken attendant who was very quick to inform us that Queen Victoria and Prince Albert often gave these exquisitely crafted and expensive works of art to each other for birthdays and Christmas.

"Well, you *do* get stuck sometimes, Mum, don't you?" Sam had commented seriously as he moved along the corridor, completely unaware of the merriment and splutters of laughter which he was leaving behind him.

And so the changes from the unselfconscious happy days of childhood continued, to be replaced by the gradual creeping of adolescence. The normal exuberant childish chatter had diminished and in its place were grunts and long silences as Sam began to grapple with growing up. My job now seemed to be one of interpreting his adolescent moods. His expectations and aspirations were changing from impatient childish demands to the slightly more sophisticated hopes and dreams of a teenage boy. While out driving recently, John commented on a particularly spectacular Honda motorbike which came whizzing up behind us.

"Now that's my idea of style!" he commented drooling at the mouth.

"It's not mine!" offered Sam. "Mine's a moped, a boy's motorbike," he declared with relish.

"You might change as you get older and want something like an Aston Martin or a Porsche," suggested John.

"No, Dad, I'll always want a moped, even when I'm old," declared Sam with such assurance that John couldn't resist the comment,

"Well that could cramp your style a bit, when you reach thirty and you're out on the town. Just imagine at the end of the evening: you lean against a Porsche and ask a girl if she would like a lift home, then when she says 'yes' walking her round the corner and showing her your moped!" He and Sam both exploded with laughter as they recalled their current favourite advert on the television. This incident made me reflect upon the importance of laughter, which had seen us through some of our most difficult times and which had proved a most invaluable tool in levering Sam out of his more difficult moods.

As I sense the passing of childhood and the shift from one stage of growing to another, I muse on the special demands that adoption places upon a family, the things which you are denied as a parent and the extra pleasures that it can bring. The sense of permanence that birth parents take for granted, the statements that seem to fall so effortlessly from the lips of friends and family.

'She's just the image of her mother, grandmother, grandfather' - the family traits and characteristics and physical appearances which reassuringly pass from one generation to the next. This loss of such delights is counterbalanced by the joy of discovering positive qualities within an adoptive child and nurturing them, thereby gaining the satisfaction of knowing that you have helped them realise their potential, whatever that may be. And, as if by osmosis, the miracle that seems to happen when you notice that some of your own mannerisms and characteristics, indeed, have been picked up, copied and internalised. On arranging a recent sleep-over with a friend at our house, Sam informed me of the sleeping arrangements, over which I couldn't help but chuckle.

"I'll let Jason sleep in my room, mum," he announced, "I'll have the futon in the playroom. I need my own space!" I instantly recognised my own middle-aged mutterings which Sam had subconsciously absorbed and seen fit to regurgitate, reminding me of the tremendous responsibility of providing a suitable role model for a child to emulate. Sam's passion for teacakes, hot chocolate and Ken Dodd meant that he would fit in nicely with any Saga holiday, which was all John's doing! The suggestion that he should go swimming in the school holidays one hot August morning was met with "I don't want to go swimming this morning, I've just washed my hair!" Me, I'm afraid!

And so the responsibility of parenthood continues. The fears and concerns for the future are there for the time when we shall have to let go and let him fend for himself in the world.

In due time we shall encourage the inevitable meetings and re-unions between Sam, his siblings and his birth parents, and we hope that these will bring him the joys and pleasures of an extended family, something which remains very important for an only child in an adoptive family. And finally, the hope that a little bit of what we have tried to teach him, about life and how to live it, will stay with him forever.

Reflections on living with a "Back-to-Front" Boy.

Looking back over the ten years we have been Sam's parents, we have come so far in some respects and yet only taken a few steps in others. I have been asked to write a section to end this book, containing thoughts and reflections on our time together.

Schools and learning.

A significant problem - which remained undiagnosed for many years - was Sam's learning difficulty. This difficulty was obscured by the emotional trauma of his early years, which we were told would cause delayed development. If we had known that Sam had this problem we would probably have been more patient and less demanding in our expectations. We were led to believe that after two years of a steady home environment he would "catch up." With hindsight, in our enthusiasm to help him make up for his unfortunate beginning, we probably placed too many unrealistic demands upon him, which could have been responsible for some of the frequent temper tantrums in the early days.

We associated his bad behaviour and developmental delay with early emotional trauma, never stopping to consider that there could be another underlying problem which was the cause. Indeed, ten years later, we are still coming to terms with his Specific Learning Difficulty, which manifests itself in dyslexic tendencies. Even though we have been told that Sam doesn't fit into the "dyslexic box" because his IQ isn't high enough, we know that whatever the problem is, Sam's short-term memory causes him real problems with his learning. For example, when trying to add two numbers together in his head, he finds it impossible to hold onto the first part of the calculation while he works out the second part. On many occasions he has been sent home from school with instructions to learn his tables, when quite clearly Sam find this almost impossible. Only the other day at a parent's evening, we were told by a young, enthusiastic maths teacher, that if children could learn their alphabet then they could learn their tables.

After four years experience of a school for children with mild learning difficulties, we feel that the teachers still do not fully understand the nature of Sam's problems and how it affects his learning. We feel that the teaching needs to be adapted to suit the individual needs of each pupil so that they are better equipped to cope in the real world. We don't expect Sam to leave school with any formal qualifications but we do expect him to be able to fill out a simple form, read a simple newspaper, check his change in a shop and hopefully, get to work on time.

People who have helped us.

We will always be grateful to Sam's first teacher, however, who showed remarkable insight and sensitivity, making his first year of schooling much less traumatic than it could have been. Her ability to set Sam appropriate challenges, both intellectually and behaviourally was superb; I just wish her skill and expertise could be bottled and distributed!

His four years of private tuition with a Dyslexia Specialist/Counsellor was also vital in helping Sam take steps forward in his learning. Her ability to tease out the next stages of his learning in a logical, sequential and non–threatening way meant that Sam viewed her as his friend as well as his teacher. An acute observer of human nature, she never actually pushed Sam too far - he was challenged but never overwhelmed, therefore helping to establish respect and trust. This in turn helped build Sam's fragile self-esteem, for which we will always be grateful.

Our experience with the DDAT Centre at Kenilworth proved a positive one. Their diagnosis of an under-developed cerebellum and their subsequent exercise programme seemed to improve Sam's sense of logic, concentration and certainly helped to calm him down.

The use of alternative medicine, although not suitable for everyone, has certainly helped us in controlling Sam's periods of aggression and outbursts of temper. It has proved cheap, reliable and so far as we know, has left no visible side effects. The care and attention that our particular homeopath has given us as a family, will always be remembered gratefully, as will his unobtrusive, calm, gentle and relaxed manner.

Respite, friends and family.

If we had known how demanding and relentless the task before us was going to be, we would have tried harder to set up a wider network of suitable respite support workers with whom we could have left Sam. Although elderly grandparents offered help frequently, Sam's challenging behaviour required a lot of understanding and energy to keep the relationship from becoming confrontational and so we were reluctant to take them up on their offer, preferring to see them with us firmly in control. Frequent breaks were needed, as children with difficulties put an enormous strain on any relationship, bringing feelings of isolation. The challenge of supporting these children can sometimes be overwhelming. There is a real need to get away and mix with good friends, and it is vital to relax and recharge batteries on a regular basis. It is amazing how a seemingly unsurmountable problem suddenly becomes less daunting and more manageable after a weekend of fun, laughter and wine!

At the beginning of this piece I said that we had come a long way in some respects but only taken a few steps in others. A recent family funeral gave me time to reflect upon this. Sam was clearly moved by the occasion and sat between John and his cousin, a girl who is exactly the same age as him. He listened intently as the various family members went to the front of the church, to read pieces from the Bible that my uncle had found comforting during his illness. Sam stood up in church and sang each of the three hymns, even though I knew he couldn't read a lot of the words. He sat quietly, observing the proceedings and was grateful for his cousin's reassurance, when she saw that he was clearly upset. He accepted her reassuring pats, the holding of his hand and her arm around his shoulders, without the aggressive struggle he would once have given to loosen her hold and reject her care.

What a contrast to ten years ago, when we had taken Sam to the same family's wedding. What a joyous occasion, when my uncle had stood proudly in the little village church to give his daughter away. The wedding was a grand affair with a marquee on the lawn in the grounds of a beautiful cottage, minor celebrities and enough champagne to float a battleship. John and I were looking forward to our first proper outing with Sam and our chance to show him off to the rest of the family.

From the minute we walked into the church to the minute we struggled to get him into the car for the long, silent journey home, Sam displayed the most anti-social behaviour John and I had ever experienced. The list was considerable: an inability to sit still, crawling under church pews, dropping hymn books, scooping up dirty Autumn leaves to throw instead of confetti, refusing to hold our hands - or anyone else's - on the short walk from the church to the reception. Refusal to sit still on a chair in the marquee, insistence on trying everyone's champagne, which had been poured for a toast by the best man - the list went on and on! It was this same best man's speech that everyone had been looking forward to, as he was a recently retired newsreader. We all listened hard to what he had to say and hung on to every well enunciated word. It was only when he got to the bit at the end of the speech when he said, "Now would you please raise your glasses," that everyone on our table realized that their glasses were already empty! They had been methodically drunk by one very hyperactive, naughty boy. Yes, I think we have come a long way!

Useful addresses

Homeopathy:
The Society of Homeopaths,
2 Artizan Road,
Northampton NN1 4HU :
www.homeopathy-soh.org

Nutrition:
Society for the Promotion of Nutritional Therapy:
http://visitweb.com/spnt

The ADD - ADHD Family Support Group UK,
93, Avon Road,
Devizes, Wiltshire SN10 1PT.

Adoption UK,
Manor Farm, Appletree Road, Chipping Warden,
Banbury, Oxfordshire, OX17 1LH;
Helpline 0870 7700 450.
www.adoptionuk.org.uk

Families For Children,
All Saints House, Harwell Street,
Plymouth, Devon. PLI 5BW.
www.familiesforchildren.org.uk

The Dyslexia, Dyspraxia & Attention Disorder Treatment Centre,
6, The Square,
Kenilworth, Warwickshire, CV8 1EB
Tel: 0845 0250 550.
www.ddat.co.uk

Printed in the United Kingdom
by Lightning Source UK Ltd.
108501UKS00001B/118